S0-ACM-084

FRANKLIN PIERCE COLLEGE

Presented to

Franklin
Pierce
College
Library

by the

National Women's Committee

TWAYNE'S WORLD AUTHORS SERIES

A Survey of the World's Literature

Sylvia E. Bowman, Indiana University

GENERAL EDITOR

MEXICO

John P. Dyson, Indiana University

EDITOR

Sor Juana Inés De La Cruz

(TWAS 144)

TWAYNE'S WORLD AUTHORS SERIES (TWAS)

The purpose of TWAS is to survey the major writers—novelists, dramatists, historians, poets, philosophers, and critics—of the nations of the world. Among the national literatures covered are those of Australia, Canada, China, Eastern Europe, France, Germany, Greece, India, Italy, Japan, Latin America, New Zealand, Poland, Russia, Scandinavia, Spain, and the African nations, as well as Hebrew, Yiddish, and Latin Classical literatures. This survey is complemented by Twayne's United States Authors Series and English Authors Series.

The intent of each volume in these series is to present a critical-analytical study of the works of the writer; to include biographical and historical material that may be necessary for understanding, appreciation, and critical appraisal of the writer; and to present all material in clear, concise English—but not to vitiate the scholarly content of the work by doing so.

Sor Juana Inés De La Cruz

By GERARD FLYNN

University of Wisconsin — Milwaukee

Twayne Publishers, Inc. :: New York

Copyright © 1971 by Twayne Publishers, Inc.

All Rights Reserved

Library of Congress Catalog Card Number: 75-120482

32868
PQ
7296
J6
2662

MANUFACTURED IN THE UNITED STATES OF AMERICA

For The People of Mexico
With Gratitude

Preface

THE purpose of this book is to introduce the reader to the Mexican playwright and poetess, Sor Juana Inés de la Cruz (1648-1695). The first chapter emphasizes her biography, the other chapters her poetry and theater. For insights into her life I have relied on one of the most charming letters in the Spanish language, her autobiographical *Respuesta a Sor Filotea (The Reply to Sor Filotea)*. It is, moreover, her one prose work of literary importance.

I have discussed Sor Juana's philosophy in nearly all of the chapters, because her works constantly refer to the vocabulary of Scholasticism. Indeed, it is the thesis of this book that Sor Juana was a woman with a strong philosophical bent, who frequently wrote some of the best lyrical and dramatic poetry of colonial Latin America. It must be added, however, that many of her verses are uninspired lines that were written for important occasions of Church and State.

The past criticism of Sor Juana has been extremely irregular: she has been the subject of many contradictory opinions, for example, a black legend on the one hand and mystical rumors on the other. I have discussed the criticism of several authors and have attempted to set the critical house in order.

This book includes several long quotations from Sor Juana's autobiographical letter, her theater, and her poetry. The quotations are in my English translation. They are unobtainable elsewhere and I hope they will give the English reader a fair idea of Sor Juana's literature. In some cases Sor Juana is quoted in the original Spanish as well as in English so that the reader who knows Spanish can study her own text.

The better poems of Sor Juana have been commented on at some length. On the other hand, I have passed over many of her verses, for example, the *romances* (verses that rhyme in assonance), which I consider wooden. The reader who wishes to do so can check my judgment by examining Volume I of Sor Juana's *Obras completas (Complete Works)* in the edition of Alfonso Méndez Plancarte. Except for the *jácara* and the Negro poetry, most of the *villancicos* (carols) have been omitted. The dramatic poetry appears in its entirety, although I have not closely examined the *loas* (dramatic poems) written for some celebrity's birthday. As for Sor Juana's one-hundred fifty pages of prose, Chapter I is largely devoted to her thirty-five page *The Reply to Sor Filotea*. I have not discussed her devotional exercises and her bizarre *Allegorical Neptune*, which she wrote to celebrate the advent of a viceroy.

The Selected Bibliography has comments on several critics of Sor Juana, which the reader can supplement with other comments in the body of the book and in the Notes and References. In reading Sor Juana I have used the four-volume *Obras completas* edited by the late Alfonso Méndez Plancarte. He is the foremost scholar of her literature.

I wish to thank my often-remembered and well-loved *maestro*, Dr. Frank Thompson, who helped me with my first studies of Sor Juana. I am grateful to the University of Wisconsin — Milwaukee for two generous research grants.

Above all, I want to mention my debt to my wife, who knows many parts of this book as well as I.

Gerard Flynn

Milwaukee, Wisconsin

Contents

Preface

Chronology

1. The Mexican Nun   11

2. The Dream   26

3. The Secular Theater   35

4. The Religious Theater   56

5. The Poetry of Sor Juana   82

6. The Alleged Mysticism of Sor Juana   99

7. Conclusion   108

Notes and References   109

Selected Bibliography   117

Index   121

Chronology

1648   Juana de Asbaje y Ramírez, born in San Miguel de Nepantla, Mexico.

1664-   The viceroyalty of Sor Juana's friends, the Marqueses de
1670   Mancera. Sor Juana became the Marquesa's maid of honor.

1667   August 14: Entered the Convent of the Discalced Carmelites of St. Joseph. November 18: Left the convent.

1669   February 24: Entered the Convent of the Order of St. Jerome. Remained there until her death.

1676-   Wrote *villancicos* (carols) for the Cathedrals of Mexico,
1691   Puebla, and Oaxaca.

1683   *Los empeños de una casa (The Trials of a Noble House)*, a play.

1689   *Amor es más laberinto (Love the Greater Labyrinth)*, a play.

1690   The *Carta atenagórica (The Athenagoric Letter)*, which attacked a 1650 sermon of the famous Portuguese Jesuit, Antonio de Vieyra. *El divino Narciso (The Divine Narcissus)*, a sacramental play.

1692   Publication of *Poemas*, Volume I. Publication of *Poemas*, Volume II. This volume includes *El sueño (The Dream)* and *Los empeños de una casa*.

1695   April 17: Died.

1700   Publication of *Fama y obras póstumas (History and Posthumous Works)*, which includes the *Respuesta a Sor Filotea (The Reply to Sor Filotea)*.

CHAPTER 1

The Mexican Nun

I The Position of Sor Juana in Latin-American Literature

NO other writer of colonial Latin America has received more praise than Sor Juana Inés de la Cruz (1648-1695). Her contemporaries called her "the tenth muse from Mexico," a nineteenth-century Spaniard said that her love poems are some of "the softest and most delicate a woman ever penned,",twentieth-century writers from three continents have compared her to Calderón, to the mystics, to the angels, and a German author has recently returned to the adulation of the seventeenth century by titling his book *Die Zehnte Muse von Mexico.*[1] This praise does not mean that the opinions concerning Sor Juana are unanimous. Frequently the opinions are not even cordial. Some interpreters of Sor Juana have taken her to be a sincere and deeply religious person, even a mystic, whereas others have taken her to be a cautious and cunning hypocrite, even a non-believer. A grave problem exists here for the literary critic.

This critical problem of what Sor Juana represents partially arises from the attitude of various generations towards Don Luis de Góngora (1561-1627), the Spanish poet. The name of Góngora was anathema for more than two centuries because of his alleged obscurity and abuse of the Spanish language. Thus, if we read an essay on Sor Juana written as late as 1892, we find that the writer (Menéndez Pelayo) praises her literature but rejects those works that make her "more inaccessible than her model," Góngora. On the other hand, if we read an essay written in the 1940's, we find that the author (Méndez Plancarte) tries to restore Góngora and insists on Sor Juana's likeness to him. There is a third position that now questions the truly Gongorist character of Sor Juana's poetry. According to this position, a person's attitude towards Góngora does not count since Sor Juana was not a Gongorist.

One way of judging Sor Juana's place in Latin-American literary history is to compare the colonial period (1492-c. 1800) with the modern period (c. 1800-1969). Such a comparison will show that the most creative writers in Latin America from 1492 to the wars of independence against Spain, were not the poets and playwrights but the historians, such as Bernal Díaz del Castillo and Garcilaso Inca de la Vega. The histories of these men form a literary monument as durable as the European seventeenth-century theater and nineteenth-century novel, but it must be said that they belong as much to the field of history as they do to literature. During the colonial period other branches of literature do not show the same verve, the same good judgment and great store of imagination as history. Of the few exceptions to this statement, the most notable is the literature of Sor Juana Inés de la Cruz.

Another key to Sor Juana's place in Latin-American literature is the question of her nationality. Although she lived in Mexico all her life, was she strictly speaking a citizen of Mexico? Or was she a citizen of Spain? Today in Mexico novelists such as Agustín Yáñez and Juan Rulfo and dramatists such as Rodolfo Usigli are uniquely Mexican rather than Spanish or Spanish American. Yáñez' town in *On the Edge of the Storm,* Yahualica, is a Mexican town about to enter the social revolution of 1910, it could be no other; Rulfo's *cacique* is a peculiarly Mexican boss who could not be mistaken for a Spanish or Peruvian *cacique;* Usigli's characters in *Crown of Darkness* strive to grasp the truth of Querétaro in 1867 and with it the Mexican reality. In contrast with these modern authors Sor Juana strikes us as being very Spanish rather than Mexican. The setting of her play *The Trials of a Noble House* is the same as the settings in the plays of her Spanish master, Pedro Calderón (1600-1681). The Fabios and Silvios who appear in her poems are Spanish figures. She also used Greek, Latin and Spanish images rather than Mexican images in her play, *Love the Greater Labyrinth,* to show the plight of Theseus who, loved by Ariadne, loves Phaedra. Usigli acknowledged a great debt to George Bernard Shaw, but his plays could never be mistaken for those of Shaw. In contrast, if Sor Juana's play *The Divine Narcissus* were anonymous it could easily be ascribed to Calderón or another Spanish playwright.

Sor Juana's works belong to the Spanish rather than the Mexican family. Her sacramental plays and her comedies are of the school of Calderón,[2] her poetry finds its inspiration in the sonnets and *liras* of the Peninsula and even in a writer such as Gaspar Gil Polo,[3] and her prose was concerned with the ecclesiastical society she lived in, which was a mirror reflection of society in Spain. The literature of Sor Juana supports the commonly held opinion that until the nineteenth century Latin-American literature was a part of Spanish literature rather than a separate body.

It is remarkable that in spite of the great attention paid to Sor Juana there was no satisfactory edition of her works until 1951-1957, when they appeared in four volumes. It is equally remarkable that the articles and books on Sor Juana have not demonstrated what one Hispanist has called "textual control of the imagination." Most "sorjuanists" have written a series of impressions that tell us more about themselves than about the Mexican nun, with the result that a kaleidoscopic slew of opinions exists by which Sor Juana becomes pantheistic, Catholic, Cartesian, Scholastic, mystical, irreligious, generous, selfish, candid, and hypocritical. Sor Juana is apt to become whatever her critics will her to be. But in the long run the only evidence that matters is the internal evidence of her own writing.

II *The Black Legend of Sor Juana*

From 1940 to 1952 a series of books appeared questioning the loyalty and religious persuasion of Sor Juana Inés de la Cruz.[4] The general image of Sor Juana presented by these books was that of a cunning woman who entered the convent in order to have a private study. She dissembled her thoughts and spoke with tongue in cheek because a clever intellectual such as she had to beware of the Inquisition and the Jesuits. She fooled both Church and State. She acted hypocritically, she disdained religion, she became a modern heretic.

This series of books has created a new black legend, a *leyenda negra sorjuanista*, which like all enthralling legends must concern the critic. The picture of a rebellious Sor Juana is indeed a romantic one; it appeals to the imagination. But it does not square with reality, for Sor Juana has left a clear testament of her religious persuasion and loyalty to the Crown in the autobiographical *Reply to Sor Filotea* and in many plays and poems; for example, in the sonnet she dedicated to Charles II in 1685.

Charles II was riding in his carriage when he saw a priest on foot carrying the Holy Eucharist. The King immediately got out of his carriage, seated the priest, and accompanied the Eucharist as if he were another man-in-waiting. In her sonnet to the King, "Oh Spanish Monarch, Highest Lord," Sor Juana says that Charles was most sovereign when he willed to subject himself to God "amongst accidents hidden." This is a reference to the transubstantiation, by which the bread retains the appearance of bread although it becomes Christ's body. Sor Juana goes on to say that the illustrious Charles V did the same thing as Charles II, to the surprise of the "Lutheran" (the Spanish word for "Protestant") and so did the great Emperor Rudolph, "who saw the world's scepter in his pious hand." The King's action has been applauded on Spanish soil, but with Catholic joy: the national acclaim of the King has been inspired by a religious, supranationalist feeling. The King's action does not suprise Sor Juana. Let him who trusts not be amazed, him who did not suppose more religion in Charles' piety, virtue and zeal.

The sonnet to Charles V was written by a Mexican nun who was conscious of her loyalty to the Spanish Church and State. Like all the other literature of this nun, it was not cunning, hypocritical, disdainful. It was written directly. It was not written with tongue in cheek.

III *Her Life*

Doña Juana de Asbaje y Ramírez de Santillana, the future nun, Sor Juana Inés de la Cruz, was born in November, 1648, and baptized on December 2 of the same year.[5] She was registered on the rolls as "a daughter of the Church" since her parents were not formally married.

Sor Juana was raised in the country at the home of her maternal grandfather, whose library was her favorite recreation. Neither punishments nor scoldings could keep her away from his books. She had learned to read when she was three years old, and at the age of six or seven she heard of the university in Mexico City and begged her mother to send her there. When she was eight years old she wrote a dramatic poem to the Eucharist. She was so eager to learn she inflicted punishments on herself that were unusual for a child her age. She refrained from eating cheese, which she liked, because she had heard that it made men stupid. She also cut her hair if she did not learn her Latin grammar:

I began to study Latin, in which I believe I took less than twenty lessons, and my concern was so strong that even though the natural adornment of hair is very important to women, especially in the flower of their youth, I would cut off two or three inches of mine after first measuring its original length. And I made a rule for myself that if my hair grew back that far without my knowing such and such a point, which I had set out to learn while the hair was growing, I was to cut off the hair again as a punishment for my ignorance. It turned out that the hair grew back and I hadn't learned what I proposed to, because the hair grew quickly and I learned slowly. As a result, I cut off the hair in punishment for my head's ignorance, for it didn't seem right to me that a head so naked of knowledge should be dressed up with hair. For knowledge is a more desirable adornment. *(Reply to Sor Filotea)*

Sor Juana knew enough Latin after twenty lessons to learn the rest of the language for herself. This autodidactic training characterized her whole life in the convent, where she studied very hard without the benefit of a teacher and fellow students. Her teacher, she once said, was always a mute book, her classmate an inkwell without feeling.

When she was sixteen Sor Juana went to the Viceroys' palace as a lady of the Marquesa de Mancera. Favorite topics of discussion at the Court that year, 1665, were the arrival of the ship from the Philippines, the death of the Archbishop, the execution of certain Indian and *mestizo* highwaymen, the arrival of the flotilla from Spain, the magician who could take things out of his mouth, the burning of a village in Holland, the expulsion of a Carmelite priest, some big hail storms, the arrival of some Capuchins, the earthquake that lasted "more than three credos," and the tightrope walker who came to Mexico at the end of December.[6] Sor Juana watched and learned the habits of the court. She was soon charming the other persons "with her genteel spirit."[7] The most charmed of all was the Viceroy's wife, the Marquesa, who urged her husband to have the professors come from the university to question Sor Juana on her knowledge. They came, some forty of them, and she defended herself "as a Royal Galley would against a few canoes."[8]

In spite of her success at the court, Sor Juana was attracted to the religious life. On the vigil of the Feast of the Assumption, 1667, she entered the Convent of the Discalced Carmelites, but she became ill there and left three months later. A year after that she entered the Order of St. Jerome (the Hieronymites). This was a trying year for Sor Juana who, even as a young woman, had clear ideas concerning her religion and her own disposition. A person with a religious calling must distinguish between the substantial truth of his religion and the accidents surrounding it. He must, moreover, take into account his own likes and dislikes. Sometimes a person who takes religious vows will have to put up with inconveniences, but other states in life, such as marriage, also have their inconveniences. They also have their truth and their accidents. Reflecting on this period of her life, Sor Juana was to write:

I became a nun because although I knew the religious state in life had many things (I mean the accessory things, not the formal ones) that were repugnant to my nature, nevertheless, owing to my total disinclination to marriage, it was the most fitting and suitable state I could elect, anxious as I was to assure my salvation. *(Reply to Sor Filotea)*

Sor Juana stayed with the Hieronymites from 1669 until her death in 1695. Mexico City during these years was a provincial capital on the periphery of events in Europe. The soldiers in New Mexico were engaged in civil war, the water drainage was causing serious aggravation, pirates were harassing the coast from Vera Cruz to Tampico, mercury shipments from Peru were not arriving in time for the silver mines, highwaymen were on every road, paper was in short supply because of hoarding, the Indians were mutinous owing to the corn shortage; these notices were the major news of the day. The public was also concerned about the flotilla and the wonderful news it brought from Europe —there was a miraculous rain of blood in Naples, the Queen was bearing another child, James II, the new king of England, was going to favor his Catholic Christian vassals. With respect to Europe, Mexico was a borderland state, on the outside looking in.

As for Sor Juana, her life was bound to the ecclesiastical calendar of the convent. She rose early in the morning to recite the first of the Canonical Hours with the other sisters. She looked forward to the great feasts of the Church and sometimes she was commissioned to write *villancicos* (church carols) for them. She cooked with the other sisters, settled arguments among the convent's many servants (there were more servants than nuns),[9] consoled the other sisters even though they came to her and interrupted her studies, accepted the counsel of her prioress, sat in the parlor for a theological discussion, served as archivist of the convent, refused an election to the office of prioress,[10] and studied whenever she had a chance. She noticed a certain tightening of the reins in conventual life when the Archbishop forbade the faithful to visit "the vestibules and railings of the convent." The Archbishop also ordered the nuns to get rid of the pet dogs in their convents, and the absence of these animals was noticeable.

From 1669 to 1690 Sor Juana studied as much as she could within the routine of her convent. She built up a library of four thousand volumes.[11] She was an ordinary nun endowed with an extraordinary intellect. In 1690 the so-called incident of the letters radically changed her way of life, so much so that in 1695, just five years later, she died an extreme ascetic with no books to her name. Her only thoughts in her last years were of God and her soul's salvation.

IV *The Incident of the Letters*

On Holy Thursday of 1650, when Sor Juana was one year old, the Portuguese Jesuit Antonio de Vieyra gave a sermon in the Royal Chapel of Lisbon on the greatest gifts or favors *(finezas)* of Christ. In his sermon Vieyra rejected the opinions of SS. John Chrysostom, Augustine, and Thomas Aquinas. Since Vieyra was the most famous orator of his day, his speech made a lasting impression.

Some forty years later, Sor Juana was engaged in a casual conversation[12] in the reception room of her convent when she praised parts of Vieyra's speech but disagreed with some of his arguments. The person she was talking to asked her to put her thoughts on paper, with the result that she addressed him a letter passing judgment on the sermon of Vieyra. She did not name the recipient of the letter, whom she merely addressed as "My dear sir," but directly or indirectly the letter came into the hands of the Bishop of Puebla, Don Manuel Fernández de Santa Cruz.

Don Manuel liked the letter so much he had it published with the title *Carta atenagórica (The Athenagoric Letter,* or, *The Letter Worthy of Minerva).* He wrote a brief letter of his own as a prologue to Sor Juana's letter and signed it with a fictitious name, Sor Filotea de la Cruz. Thus the bishop wrote as if he were one nun addressing another. In her *Reply to Sor Filotea,* Sor Juana is in reality writing to the august Bishop of Puebla.

In his pseudonymous *Letter from Sor Filotea de la Cruz,* Don Manuel had said to Sor Juana: "I have seen your letter and admired your proofs and the clarity of your argument. Consequently I have had your letter printed. Now I should like to make some suggestions. You have a great talent and although I do not suggest you stop reading books, I do suggest you read more about Christ Our Lord. I do not agree with those who say that women should not be learned. St. Jerome certainly approved of their learning, and in spite of the fact that St. Paul said women should not preach, he did not say they should not learn. I suggest you continue your studies, but you ought to better the books you read, for knowledge should enlighten us and lead us toward salvation. Subordinate profane letters to sacred letters: you must study the latter more." The bishop dated his letter November 25, 1690.

Three months later, on March 1, 1691, Sor Juana answered the Bishop of Puebla with her *Reply to Sor Filotea de la Cruz.* Her reply has two main ideas: (1) "this, my black inclination" *(inclinación*—fondness, bent, love, inclination) and (2) *Mulieres in ecclesia taceant.*

By her black inclination Sor Juana means a tremendous thirst for knowledge, an overpowering tendency to read, a yearning to know more if only to be less ignorant. She must study all the time and when there are no books at hand she will learn something somehow; she will examine the beams of a ceiling to see why they converge and go down, or at least appear to do so, as they go away; she will fry one egg in oil and another in syrup, to learn that the one unites whereas the other breaks up; she will put sifted flour under a spinning top to observe its spiral path; or she will meditate, metaphysically, on the multitude of different characters who share the one human nature. She herself does not use the term, but owing to her black inclination she is an intellectual.

The *Mulieres in ecclesia taceant,* the second idea she wants to impress the bishop with, means "Let women be quiet in church," and by extension the phrase could mean "Women should be seen and not heard," or "Books, study, and learning are not for women." Sor Juana spends a good deal of time on this question, and many look upon her as the first champion of women's rights; one critic goes so far as to say "that we might well consider it *(The Reply to Sor Filotea)* the Magna Carta of intellectual liberty for women in America."[13]

The Reply to Sor Filotea is a carefully reasoned work that tells modern readers a great deal about Sor Juana's life. Sor Juana knows that Sor Filotea is the bishop (see the last two paragraphs of the letter) and she discreetly builds up a case for her two principal ideas: her own inclination towards letters and women's freedom to cultivate them.

She says she is grateful to Sor Filotea for publishing her letter on Vieyra, although she had no idea it was going to be in print. Had she known, she would have exercised more care in writing it. She agrees with Sor Filotea that she should read more sacred literature, and she will do so although one must exercise a certain caution with books such as the erotic Song of Songs, which learned men did not read before they were thirty. Sor Juana displays a gentle humor in writing to Sor Filotea, for the *Reply to Sor Filotea,* in which she promises to read more sacred literature, is filled with arguments, allusions, and Latin quotations that show how well she knew Holy Writ, the Fathers of the Church, the medieval Scholastics, and the religious writers of her own day.

Sor Juana says that in all her life as a nun she never wrote anything at her own urging except perhaps the little paper called *The Dream.* She always wrote "under duress and violence," that is, at the behest of others. She says she doesn't study to write and much less to teach, but rather because she has the craze and inclination to study and wants to be less ignorant. The inclination towards books persist even though she has tried to check it; and once when she was ill the doctors forbade her reading in the hope that this would alleviate her distress, but she had to return to her books since without them she became worse.

She tells Sor Filotea that she learned to read when she was three. In her own words:

To continue the story of my inclination, which I want you to know all about, I say that I was not yet three years old when my mother sent an older sister of mine to learn to read at one of the schools called *Amigas*, and partly out of affection, partly out of mischief, I followed her; and when I saw that they were giving her a lesson, I became so inflamed in my desire to learn how to read that I told the teacher, whom I thought I was deceiving, that my mother wanted me to have a lesson. She did not believe it, since it was unbelievable, but in a spirit of good-natured fun she gave me the lesson. I kept going and she kept teaching me, but it was no longer in fun since experience had taught her otherwise; and I learned to read in such a short time that I already knew how before my mother found out, because the teacher had kept it from her in order to surprise her and to receive a reward for her services; and I kept quiet about it, thinking they would spank me for doing it without their permission. The one who taught me is still living (may God keep her) and she can testify to what I say.

Sor Juana says that, as a very young girl, she refrained from eating cheese because someone had told her that cheese makes one stupid. She was six or seven years old when she heard of the university and schools where people studied different subjects and she wanted desperately to go to them, but since she couldn't she took care of her desire by reading the books her grandfather had. About this time she started to learn Latin grammar and in order to goad herself she would cut off her hair if she didn't know her lesson.[14]

After describing her efforts to learn Latin, Sor Juana writes some twenty-two lines that are the most important part of the *Reply*. They tell the reader a great deal about her religious life, her attitude toward marriage, her studies, and her philosophy. Here are the lines (*Entréme religiosa porque . . .*):

I became a nun because although I knew the religious state in life had many things ((I mean the accessory things not the formal ones) that were repugnant to my nature, nevertheless, owing to my total disinclination to marriage, it was the most fitting and suitable state I could elect, anxious as I was to assure my salvation. My petty whims were such that I would have preferred to live alone, to have no duty

or occupation that might interfere with my freedom for study, to
avoid the noise of a community about me which might upset the
silence of my books: this was my whim, but whim had to bow down
and subject itself to the most important of all: salvation. I vacillated
for some time in my determination, but finally some learned persons
showed me how my whims were a temptation; I conquered them
with divine help and took up the state I now so unworthily hold. I
thought I was fleeing from myself when I entered the convent but
wretch that I am I brought myself with me and I also brought my
worst enemy in this inclination to letters which (I am not certain)
was sent by Heaven either as a gift or a punishment; for instead of
dying down or going out amidst all my religious practices, it blew up
like powder and I was a living proof of the refrain *privatio est causa
appetitus.*

This passage is based on the doctrine of a vocation to a state
in life. Sor Juana says she was not attracted to the accessories, or
accidents, of conventual life, particularly the noise a community
might make at the very time she wanted to study; nevertheless,
she knew she would have to put up with these annoyances. This
was the price she had to pay for living in a religious community.
(Sor Juana's attitude should not be hard for modern teachers to
understand. Just as she liked the communal life with its religious
services, canonical hours, and collective prayer but disliked certain customs within the community, so, many teachers today like
their students and subject matter but dislike certain accessories,
for example, a meeting with the PTA, the Milk Fund, and so
forth.)

Sor Juana mentions her "total disinclination to marriage." These
rather strong words have led zealous critics to look for all sorts
of autobiographical information in Sor Juana's poetry: an unknown lover who disappointed her, or even evidence of her own
masculinity. This type of criticism has not borne good fruit. Until
some scholar comes up with new documents, the reader must con-
clude that Sor Juana had a seventeenth-century vocation to the
religious rather than the married state in life.

After speaking of her vocation Sor Juana says that she hoped
to study the queen of the sciences, Theology. But to know the
queen one must also know the handmaids, the ancillary sciences,
and so she set out to study Logic, Rhetoric, Physics, Arithmetic,
Geometry, Architecture, History, Law, Music, and Astronomy.[15]

Her inclination, she says, was general rather than particular; she was not what people today call a specialist. Sor Juana unquestionably had the thirst of a humanistic scholar.

Perhaps the most moving part of *The Reply to Sor Filotea* is the passage in which Sor Juana says she always lacked a teacher and fellow students. Whether she liked it or not she was a self-taught philosopher:

What might excuse me is the great difficulty I have had, not only in lacking a teacher but in lacking fellow students with whom to discuss and work on the subject matter. My only teacher was a mute book, my only fellow student an inkwell without feeling; and instead of explanations and exercises I had a great many interruptions, not only those of my religious duties (and these indeed are profitable and useful and do not waste time) but those that are accessory to a community; for example, I would be reading and in the next cell they would decide to play music and sing; I would be studying and two maids would have a squabble and come to me to settle their argument; or I would be writing and a friend would come to visit me, thereby doing me a bad deed with a good will—naturally I could not only show no annoyance, I had to be grateful for the harm done me. And this went on continuously, since the free hours I had for study were also the free hours of the whole community, and so the other sisters could come to interrupt me. Only those who have experienced community life know how true this is and only the strength of my vocation could make me be good-natured, that and the great love that exists between me and my beloved sisters, for love is union and where it is there are no opposite extremes.

The rest of Sor Juana's *Reply to Sor Filotea* shows that she met a great deal of opposition to her studies. Curiously, the worst opposition of all came from those who were her friends and wanted her to stop studying for her own good; for example, there was a good but unlettered prioress who looked upon studies as something to be investigated by the Inquisition. She forbade Sor Juana her studies, and during the three months she was the superior Sor Juana did not read a book. As a matter of fact, since Sor Juana could not quiet her intellect and had to apply it to something, it was during this period that she made observations of a scientific nature.

Some of the opposition, however, was not so charitable and here Sor Juana, rather than name her adversaries, contents her-

self with pointing out the example of Christ. The more He did,
the more He gave, the more He was (Sor Juana identifies perfection with being), the more He was persecuted. And so it
must be with others. The more they stand out the more they will
wear a crown of thorns, as their Savior did before them. Opposition and persecution are not to be wondered at, they are to be
expected.

Within the problem of opposition to Sor Juana comes the question of St. Paul's *Mulieres in ecclesia taceant* ("Let women be
quiet in church"), a phrase that some people employed to
discourage women from learning. Sor Juana acts as a lawyer for
the defense and draws up a formidable argument citing learned
women from Jewish and pagan antiquity and then from Chris-
tianity itself: Ste. Catherine of Egypt, Ste. Gertrude, Ste. Paula,
Ste. Theresa of Avila, and others. Sor Juana concludes that women
who have the ability for letters should study in private but not
preach in public. She also says that unqualified men would do
better not to study, for a little bit of learning is dangerous. It is
like a sword in the hands of a madman. Witness the example
of the heresiarchs!

Part of Sor Juana's argument defending woman's right to study
belongs to the biblical science called exegesis. Concerning the
Mulieres in ecclesia taceant, she holds that St. Paul meant women
could not preach from the pulpit in church although they could
study in private. She quotes parts of the Bible in favor of women's
learning and shows by many examples that one cannot place a
literal interpretation on every passage of Holy Writ. Why, then,
did the great apostle, Paul, say *Mulieres in ecclesia taceant?*
Sor Juana answers:

Moreover, that prohibition concerned a historical question which
Eusebius refers to, namely, that in the early Church women began
to preach doctrine to one another in the temples; and this noise
caused confusion while the apostles were preaching, so that the
women were ordered to be silent. And the same thing happens today,
namely, that while the preacher is preaching, one should not pray out
loud.

Sor Juana closes *The Reply to Sor Filotea* by saying she has
written two devotional works that were published without her
name. She was happy to see them published and she encloses

two copies for Sor Filotea (the bishop) to read. Otherwise she has written nothing for publication, least of all *The Athenagoric Letter*.

The Reply to Sor Filotea is the work of an intellectual who has taught herself the rudiments of many subjects and has closely examined two, philosophy and theology. She is a religious woman who, unlike many Catholics of her day, does not use her faith as an excuse for neglecting her reason. She realizes that arguments based on authority are usually the weakest arguments of all, but she will defer to authority in order to avoid scandal and to increase charity. She is an apostle of union, an enemy of discord. "For love is union and knows no opposite extremes."[16]

Sor Juana's *Reply to Sor Filotea* is "perhaps the most charming autobiography we have in the Spanish language, where this genre is so wanting."[17] Every person who is interested in Sor Juana will want to read it several times.

V *The Last Years*

The events following the incident of the letters are not clear to us today for there is very little documentary evidence to go on. We know that there was disagreement within the Church over the letters: the Bishop Manuel Fernández de Santa Cruz favored Sor Juana, whereas her own confessor, the Jesuit Father Núñez, chided her and left her. We also know that the lustrum 1690-1695 was a trying period of pestilence, hunger and insurrection, in which the Indian uprising of 1692 was the most memorable event of the time. Finally, we know that Sor Juana made a total renunciation of the world. Thus we have the general picture and the specific act of renunciation, that is to say, we have certain facts. But the causes behind these facts are not obvious. It is too much to say, as some critics have zealously asserted, that Sor Juana was the victim of a Jesuit conspiracy, or of her own menopause. There is no textual evidence to support these theories.

The fact is that after the incident of the letters, in a city suffering from pestilence and violence, this middle-aged woman sold her entire library together with her mathematical and musical instruments and destined the money to the poor. For herself she kept "three little prayerbooks and many hairshirts and disciplines." With her own blood she signed a renewal of her vows, in which she affirmed that "my lady the Virgin Mary was conceived without stain of original sin." Her confessor returned to her and now changed his role, endeavoring to restrain her rather than oppose her. The last two years, 1693-1695, are a mystery. Finally an epidemic struck the convent and Sor Juana, helping the other sisters who were older and more infirm than she, "became sick through charity." She received the sacraments and died on April 17, 1695.

In the twilight age of an old Europe, Sor Juana represented the harmony of faith and reason. She had an unusual desire to know, almost for the sake of knowing, but she tempered this desire with love and a willingness to listen to others. Reason by itself is one-sided. Faith by itself is one-sided. But Sor Juana kept an open mind. She was a true intellectual and a living example of St. Paul's letter to the Corinthians, which contains her proper epitaph:

Brethren, if I speak with the tongue of men and of angels and have not charity, I am nothing.

CHAPTER 2

The Dream

I El sueño (The Dream)

THE knowledge of men and of angels, which was an epistemological question dear to the heart of Sor Juana, is the subject of her longest poem, *El Sueño (The Dream)*, 975 verses. Apparently this poem was her favorite, for she says in *The Reply to Sor Filotea:* "I do not recall having written anything for my own pleasure except a little paper they call *The Dream.*" Although Sor Juana is exaggerating here in an effort to show she was constantly writing at the behest of others rather than at her own urging, there can be no doubt that a strange poetical probing of the nature of human thought would appeal to her.

II *The Meaning of* The Dream

The meaning of Sor Juana's poem *The Dream* may be considered from two points of view: the story it tells and the philosophy underlying that story.

The story of Sor Juana's *Dream* is rather clear. Night rises up from the earth to the moon and rules the atmosphere. Great nocturnal birds, including bats, who are featherless birds, come and create a darkness within a darkness. Everything must sleep, the fish, the beasts, the birds, the robber, the lover—everything. It is the *conticinio,* the hour of total silence.

The body sleeps as in death and the soul no longer has to exercise its external government. Phantasy begins to trace the images of all things on the earth and in the spheres, things material and immaterial, visible and invisible. The soul feels as free as an angel, a disembodied spirit, and strives to intuit its own being and the being of the universe. The soul stands aloft on a mountain higher than Mt. Atlas and Mt. Olympus, which do not even come up to its slopes. The very eagle who drinks the rays of the sun cannot fly up to this great mountain. The soul is above the world and can look at all creation.

But the soul is not equal to the task. Just as the eye, whose proper object is light, cannot look at the sun without being blinded, so the soul cannot contemplate the cosmos without losing its sight. In trying to see everything the soul sees nothing, it is stupefied by so many species.

An eye blinded by the sun seeks darkness, where it may see again. Similarly, the soul flees the cosmos for a more modest ground. Like a ship with broken mast and shattered rudder, it seeks the "mental shore." It will kiss each grain of sand, it will look at one thing at a time. It will use the ten categories since it cannot know all of creation in one intuitive act. It will follow the scale of being, it will examine the mineral, vegetable, and animal worlds.

The soul cannot understand the simple things of this world, a fountain, a lily, a rose. How then can it ever hope to understand, by one intuitive glance, the cosmos and all of Nature? There was indeed a youth who tried to drive the chariot of the sun, but his example is not to be followed.

The body starts to wake up now. The eyes open, the senses recover, and the brain is free of the phantasms of the dream. The sun does battle with the night, who, like all cowards, flees before him. The sun arrives and impartially gives its rays to all. The world is lighted and "I am awake." (The poetess wakes up. Thus far, the story of her dream.)

The story of Sor Juana's *Dream* may be reduced to a few short statements: the world falls asleep, the poetess dreams, her soul is almost free of her body, it sees fantastic things, it tries to intuit all being, it cannot do so, it must look at things one by one, day comes, the poetess wakes up. This story is rather easy to narrate. But what is the philosophical meaning behind this story?

Sor Juana's *Dream* is an Aristotelian-Thomistic explanation of the nature of human knowledge. Man is higher than the other animals, whose knowledge is restricted to the evidence of the senses, and lower than the angels, those pure spirits who by their nature intuit the reality of things. Man is a "triple composition" (v. 655) since in addition to his own rational nature he possesses the natures of the plants and animals; but man's animal condition is a "haughty baseness" (v. 694) for through his intellect he can rise above all visible creation. Thus he is the hinge that links the material and spiritual worlds (v. 659), and the seat of that "amorous union" (v. 699) by which the Word, Christ, became flesh.[1]

If man has a low estate, like the plants and animals, he also has a dignity comparable to that of the angels. He must not, however, take himself to be an angel, for that is an act of pride worthy of a Phaeton, who attempted to steer the sun. A man who attempts to intuit the spheres as if he were an angel (vv. 297-302) will find that he must rush down from his high mountain and return to the mental shore (v. 566). What is that mental shore? It is the evidence of the senses and discursive reasoning. Man abstracts his ideas from sense evidence for "there is nothing in the intellect that was not first in the senses."[2] Man cannot intuit everything at once. His intellect is not equal to the charge. Nor can he really know simple things, one fountain, one lily, one rose. Individual objects escape his definition. But he is able to consider things one at a time, abstract universal ideas (v. 588) from his sense data, and so have a glimpse into the essence of things. He can use the ten categories of Aristotle (v. 582). In a word, he can reason discursively (v. 579), as indeed he must for it is his nature to do so.

In keeping with her Scholastic training, Sor Juana held the idea of God the First Cause, Nature the secondary cause and a natural law uninterrupted by God in its operation. Her poem tells us that man has to be true to his own nature for if he tries to act beyond it he will suffer metaphysical inundations that will keep him in his natural state.

The meaning of Sor Juana's *Dream* brings to mind two outstanding works of the seventeenth century, Calderón's *Life Is a Dream* (1635) and Pascal's *Thoughts* (1658-1662). Both of these authors also see a duality in man. Calderón's vision is dramatically religious: man is a king and a beast, a noble figure who must return to dust because of original sin, a being who dreams that the glories of this world are real, only to wake up in death to see the real reality. Pascal's vision is intuitively and scientifically religious (the paradox of *finesse* and *géométrie* is Pascal's): shaken by the winds, rising above the stars, lost in the Fall, redeemed by God, man is both great and mean, high and low, he is a thinking reed. Sor Juana's vision is primarily philosophical: a fellow creature of angels and beasts, aspiring to the heavens and wedded to earth, by nature a "haughty baseness," man cannot

attempt to intuit the cosmos at one fell stroke but must reason
discursively, from humble things to those on high.

Sor Juana is not the peer of Calderón or Pascal, whose writings
belong to the first rank of world literature. It must be said,
however, that she has left us a delightful and amazing poem in
The Dream, which throws light on the ambiguous man of the
seventeenth century.

III   *The Form of* The Dream

If *The Dream* contained nothing more than the ideas in the
summary above it would be the subject of a philosophical study
rather than a study in literature. But it has much more to offer.
It has other shades of meaning taken from the mythology and
science of Sor Juana's day, and formal aspects that are the subject of the present discussion.

The Dream has a strange effect on the reader. It reads as if
one were travelling in a straight line, a rigorously logical line,
that gives way at irregular intervals to whirlpools and eddies;
nevertheless, one has the impression on finishing it of having
travelled in a vast orbit, rather like the earth in its path around
the sun. Indeed, the poem begins with the coming of night and
ends with the victory of the dawn.

The poem begins with a description of the night, which is
not referred to by its name but as a "pyramidal, gloomy of the
earth/ born shade." Night, the first principal idea of the poem,
taks up the first sixty-four verses. The movement of the poem is
linear in its meaning but circular in its form. Verses 1-18 present
the night, verses 19-38 introduce the owl who personifies the
night, and verses 39-64 intensify the darkness of the night through
other nocturnal creatures, especially bats. Within each of these
groups of verses we find other images that seem to divagate, only
to return to the theme of night. Thus the opening of the poem
gives the impression of a line, the night, with volutes and other
adornments so minute that the reader is amazed. This amazement
confirms one scholar's judgment of that Baroque art to which Sor
Juana's poem belongs: "To amaze and be amazed were a part of
the conscious program of Baroque poetics."[3]

The opening verses describe the night: "A pyramidal, gloomy of
the earth/ born shade, to the Heavens lifted/ of vain obelisks
the haughty point/ with the hope of mounting to the stars." On

the one hand the night is a massive, dismal object, a black
pyramid; on the other, it is not a monolith but a phenomenon
with many sharp and penetrating aspects (vain obelisks). The
first small turn of the poem then follows—the distant stars scoff
at the dark war of the night; and then the second, which is based
on mythology—the dense breath of the shadow does not reach
as far as the three-faced goddess, the moon. Sor Juana does not
mention the moon or the night by name. One is the three-faced
goddess, the other the earth-born shade.

The night has been seen from without. Now it must be seen
from within. The next verses introduce the owl *(lechuza):* "the
shameless Nictimene lies spying/ each crevice of the sacred
doors/ or of the skylight eminent/ the most propitious aperture."
Sor Juana does not mention the owl by name. Nictimene, a maid
of Lesbos who sinned in her father's bed, was changed into an
owl as punishment.[4]

In this dark night there are still some faint beams of light
eerily straining their way through the cracks in the church sky-
lights and doors; *church* is not mentioned, but only *sacred doors;*
nothing is mentioned in itself if some indirect turn of phrase is at
hand. This church with its towers is an eminent structure in the
night. Nictimene waits at the apertures for her chance to snuff
out the source of light, "which she extinguishes if she does not
desecrate."[5] Nictimene, the phlegmatic owl in this night of black
vapors, may extinguish the lights with those heavy wings or, as
an alternative, if her heavy spirit moves her, she may consume
the oil of the lamps.

This last image belongs to the poetic act known as the exaltation of nature in the age of Góngora.[6] The poet does not say that
Nictimene will drink the oil but that she will "consume the liquid
which after great complaint is sweated and wrung from the fruit
of Minerva's tree." This translation is not complete. The Spanish
phrases *de prensas agravado* and *congojoso sudó y rindió forzado*
personify the olive as if it were a taxpayer who had been put on
the rack. The oil of the lamps is transformed into something
marvelous, which the exalted owl consumes.

The next verses (39-64) are variations on the theme of night
that intensify the darkness. Nictimene has stilled the church
lights because a chorus of birds comes forth that is blacker than
night itself. Once again the verses, which owe a specific debt to

the *Metamorphoses* of Ovid, are mythological. Sor Juana does not refer to bats as such. Since they are not a part of nature suitable to her vision, they must be transformed into the precious metal of poetry. The bats are the three sisters who chose to go on with their weaving and story-telling rather than pay homage to Bacchus. The wrathful god changed their cloth into vines and they themselves into birds without feathers, naked birds, with brown membranes, birds who cannot sing, birds who will no longer tell stories. These sisters are more nocturnal than the night itself: "a second shade they form/ fearing to be seen even in the darkness." They are joined by another creature who is not called an owl *(buho)* but "the once talkative minister of Pluto, now the superstitious sign for soothsayers"; he is Ascalafo, who was changed into an owl for having told on Prosperina. This gruesome crew of night birds forms a frightful chorus, for which the involved syntax of the verses is well suited.

In spite of all the twists and turns of the opening verses (1-64), Sor Juana has made only one statement that is carried on into the story of the poem: *It is night.* In making this statement, she never calls a spade a spade: the moon is a three-faced goddess, churches are sacred doors, an owl is a Nictimene or a superstitious sign for soothsayers. Sor Juana must alter, intensify, and elevate the reality before her.[7]

The next group of verses (65-150) gives the effects of night. Sor Juana is always logical. Night is a cause that has its effects: "it brought on sleep," "it induced peace," "it invited rest." Finally she sums up all the effects of night: "sleep in short possessed all." The poem has now made two statements. *It is night. The world has gone to sleep.*

Once again we wish to know how Sor Juana has handled her theme. In saying that the world has gone to sleep her verses differ somewhat from the previous pattern of night-owl-nocturnal creatures. In the first pattern she used the owls and the birds to stress the theme of night. Now she sets up a rather free order in nature to show a comatose, dreamy world.[8] Sor Juana pictures all of nature asleep, the wind and the sea, the fishes and the kingfisher, the highland beasts and the stag, the birds and the eagle. For her poetic purpose, she uses the composition known as the *silva,* a series of verses in which eleven-syllable lines appear alone or accompanied by seven-syllable lines; these verses

may or may not rhyme and they are grouped freely without any
strophaic order.[9] The *silva,* in which the author can increase
the depth of the poem by increasing the number of eleven-syllable
lines, is an excellent vehicle for a poem about a dream. A dream
in fact is rather like a *silva,* which rhymes here and there, as if
capriciously, and is now more dense, now more light and airy.
A dream, like a *silva,* is undetermined.

In one verse, "The wind calmed, the hound asleep," Sor Juana
abandons the art of *The Dream.* She has taken the trouble to
establish the order in nature of stream, fish, beast, bird, and here
she breaks it, apparently only to fill out a line (in Spanish this
is called a *ripio).* In the following verse she says that the hound
is reclining.[10] But he never appears again in the poem, with the
result that he breaks the precedent established in Nictimene the
owl, the three bats who are sisters, and the other creatures that
come after: this hound is an unexalted animal.

In the *silva* a poet can move leisurely and explore many
avenues. Thus Sor Juana does not give the order of stream-fish-
beast-bird in a strict 1-2-3-4 or 4-3-2-1 fashion (as a dramatic poet
such as Calderón does in *Life Is a Dream),* but in a labyrinthine
winding from 1 to 2, then 3 to 4. The wind does not move its
atoms lest it make a sacrilegious noise breaking the slumbersome
silence and the sea does not move "the unstable cerulean crib"
where the sun sleeps. The wind does not do one thing and the
sea does not do another. Inanimate matter is at rest.

The poem passes now to animate beings. The sleeping, forever
mute fish are doubly mute in the muddy couches of their obscure
cavernous depths, while the deceitful charmer Alcione, who
ordinarily hunts fish, now slumbers with them. The fish, silent
by nature, are now silent by sleep. They are joined by the Alcione
of myth, the siren who used to charm her lovers and entwine them
in nets as if they were fish; she was later transformed into a
bird, the kingfisher. Alcione has become not only a bird but
through sleep a silent fish.

The soporific beasts are pictured in general and then par-
ticularized in the lion, who is king, and the stag, who used to be
Ovid's hunter, Aceton. As for the birds, the light throng slumbers
in its unstable hammock and Jupiter's majestic fowl, the eagle,
sleeps perched on one foot with a stone held in the other. This
stone is "the alarm clock of his dream." There is also an apos-
trophe on the cares of majesty.

We seem to have come a long way, with pyramids to the moon, owls in churches, soporific bats, motionless winds, fishes in the deep, beasts in the mountain, the eagle on high; nevertheless, only two things have been said in the story of the poem: (1) it is night and (2) the world is asleep. This is indeed the Gongorist exaltation of nature, which characterizes the first 150 verses of *The Dream.*

A close reading of *The Dream* will show that it falls into two divisions, verses 1-150 and verses 151-975. Poetically speaking, the first division is by far the better of the two; as a matter of fact, the second division is more interesting for its philosophical argument than its poetry. We have already discussed this philosophical argument above, in "The Meaning of *The Dream.*"

To sum up, verses 1-150 tell the reader that night has fallen and the world has gone to sleep. The emphasis is on the form of the poem, which exalts the simple statement of a slumbering world. The opening verses do not convey any of the philosophical meaning of *The Dream.*

On the other hand, verses 151-975 may be considered to be an entirely different poem. Here the exaltation of nature is not the author's principal end, and indeed it is difficult to see how it could be, given Sor Juana's reliance on the vocabulary of Scholasticism and the peculiar science of her day. In the second division, or poem, Sor Juana abandons the mythology and indirect imagery of the prelude; she occasionally makes a brief halt and a gesture back towards the beginning of the poem, but her philosophical argument will permit no more than that. As we have seen, the argument of the second part boils down to an old Scholastic maxim: "There is nothing in the intellect that was not first in the senses." Man must reason discursively.

IV   *Past Criticism of* The Dream

The Dream will serve as a good example of the rather confused state of sorjuanista criticism, until the late Alfonso Méndez Plancarte (1909-1955) entered the picture and set the house in order. There is still a great deal of work to be done on Sor Juana, but all critics will acknowledge a debt to this indefatigable scholar.

Sor Juana herself may have favored *The Dream*, but it was not generally well received until the twentieth century. The critics

of the eighteenth century did not take kindly to its fantastic,
Gongorist character, and this attitude prevailed until the end of
the nineteenth century, when Marcelino Menéndez y Pelayo
(1856-1912) wrote the following words in his *History of Hispano-
American Poetry:* "To be sure they admired Sor Juana much
more when in her phantasy of *The Dream* she set out to imitate
the *Solitudes* of Góngora, becoming more incomprehensible than
her model . . ."[11] Menéndez y Pelayo praised several of her other
works, but he reared up short at what he conceived to be an
imitation of the Baroque poet, Góngora.

The critics of the twentieth century have praised *The Dream*,
but their interpretations of the poem show a singular lack of
agreement. Ermilo Abreu Gómez looked upon her thought in
The Dream as Cartesian. Ezequiel Chávez constŕued her thought
to be a peculiar quasi-pantheistic angelism[12] by which she could
soar to the Great Beyond *(Más Allá)*, and, structurally speaking,
he broke up *The Dream* into six divisions. Ludwig Pfandl likened
The Dream to a Gothic altar, "consisting of a central dominating
block and a double set of lateral wings,"[13] and he broke it up
into five divisions, not six. Pfandl's prose translation of *The
Dream* is faithful as a literal rendition of the poem, but he does
not understand Sor Juana's philosophical or theological references;
for example, he misses the point in the "amorous union" of
verses 698-99. Another critic, Karl Vossler, throws a great deal
of light on Sor Juana's poem in his essay *The World in The
Dream*, but he mistakes her philosophical attitude when he says:
"Her poem takes in with all the freshness of a youthful and
virginal desire the wisdom of Egypt, the ancient myths, the
Ptolemaic concept of the world, Aristotle, St. Thomas Aquinas,
Harvey, the ideas of Plato, and the magical lantern of Athanasius
Kircher."[14] Sor Juana unquestionably had a childlike zeal when
it came to knowledge, but this zeal is not the stuff of *The Dream*.
As a matter of fact, *The Dream* makes an extremely sober and
absolute philosophical statement.

Alfonso Méndez Plancarte, who so fondly edited *The Complete
Works of Sor Juana*, was the first of her critics to catch the
epistemological meaning of *The Dream*. On philosophical grounds
he divided the story of the poem into twelve parts, whereas on
formal grounds we have divided it into two parts. Both divisions
are admissible.

CHAPTER 3

The Secular Theater

I *The Theater*

THE *Dream, The Reply to Sor Filotea,* some sonnets, and
the poem in defense of women, "Hombres necios que
acusáis," are the best-known works of Sor Juana. They are
mentioned in every literary history or included in every anthology.
Nevertheless, she was at her best when writing for the theater.
It seems that modern criticism has generally ignored Sor Juana's
theater because a comedy such as *Los empeños de una casa
(The Trials of a Noble House)* is suited to a seventeenth-century
rather than a twentieth-century audience, and a sacramental play
such as *El divino Narciso (The Divine Narcissus)* is beyond the
pale of modern taste.

Sor Juana's theater may be divided into two categories, the
secular and the religious. In this chapter we shall consider the
secular theater and in Chapter IV the religious theater.

The secular theater of Sor Juana consists of two comedies of
entanglement, two one-act intermezzos or skits *(sainetes),* fourteen
dramatic poems *(loas),* nearly all of which celebrate the birthday
of a prominent person, and one soiree *(sarao).* Many of these
pieces were presented together in what the Spaniards of the
seventeenth century called a festival *(festejo);* for example,
in the fall of 1683 Mexico City saw the festival of *The Trials of
a Noble House,* which included, in order, a dramatic poem
preceding the comedy, a poem to be sung to the Viceroy's wife,
the first act of the play *The Trials of a Noble House,* another
poem for the Viceroy's wife, the first one-act intermezzo, the
second act of the play, a poem to the Viceroy's young son, the
second one-act intermezzo, the third and last act of the play,
and finally the soiree of the four nations. The unity of all these
theatrical pieces is external rather than internal since they were
presented together only as a social celebration paying homage

to the viceroys. Consequently the various pieces may be examined separately without damage to their character as literature.[1]

II   Los empeños de una casa (The Trials of a Noble House)

A *comedia de enredo* is a three-act play filled with entanglements designed to amaze the audience and, in some cases, to make it laugh. It usually has an almost mathematical balance of characters, which survives the entanglements until the *desenredo,* or denouement, near the end of the third act. The balance of characters gives a certain symmetry to the play and enables the audience to steer its way through the confusion. *The Trials of a Noble House* is a *comedia de enredo.*

Don Pedro and Doña Ana are a brother and sister who love Doña Leonor and Don Carlos. Their love, however, is unrequited since Doña Leonor and Don Carlos love each other. Here is a graphic representation of this entanglement:

Brother and sister	Their loves	However, these two love each other
Pedro and Ana	Leonor and Carlos	Leonor and Carlos

There are several symmetries that stem from this relationship of the two ladies and two gentlemen. The servant of Doña Ana has a counterpart in the servant of Don Carlos; they are Celia and Chestnut, who with their crude mercenary love, their selfishness, and their plays on words stand in contrast to Doña Leonor and Don Carlos with their ideal love.

There is another symmetry in the position of Ana's brother, Don Pedro, and Leonor's father, Don Rodrigo. Pedro jealously guards the reputation of his sister and himself. His role of honor-guardian is balanced by Leonor's father, Don Rodrigo, who jealously protects her honor and his own:

Pedro (brother)	guard	Ana (sister)
Rodrigo (father)		Leonor (daughter)

There is, moreover, a symmetry in the positions of the servants. Don Rodrigo has a loyal servant in Hernando, whose faithfulness finds its opposite in the treachery of Doña Ana's servant, Celia.

There is still another symmetry when two men take opposite positions in their use of force. Don Rodrigo will protect Leonor's honor even if he must use force (his sword); Don Juan, a suitor of Ana, will bring her to bed even if he must use force (rape). Typical of this kind of play is an entanglement *(enredo)* that

consists of a mistake in identity: the scene in which Don Juan
tries to force himself on Doña Ana takes place in the dark and
it is really Doña Leonor on whom he makes his advances; thus
Don Juan opposes his force to that of Don Rodrigo.

There are other symmetries too numerous and complicated for
description here. Sor Juana constantly presents them to the
audience, for repetitious situations are characteristic of the
comedias de enredo.

III *The* gracioso

The *gracioso* of Sor Juana is similar to the *gracioso* that
Calderón has created in his plays. Chestnut is fond of making
puns, and when he does Don Carlos chides him: "Keep quiet,
fool!" There is never any doubt in the minds of the other
characters that the *gracioso* is an inferior being. He is a fool.[2]

When the *gracioso* makes love to a servant girl there is no
doubt in their own minds that they are inferior:

CELIA
I have told you not to love me.
CHESTNUT
Then what does your harshness want
if I cannot escape
my imprisonment and your love?
But since you are a servant, how come you are so proud?
CELIA
A servant he calls me? The wretch! (Act I, vv. 173-78)

Chestnut is readily frightened and he is a coward (Act II,
vv. 639-44; Act II, vv. 694-99), but even when frightened he is an
opportunist who would have his master marry for money (Act I,
vv. 630-31; Act I, vv. 648-56).

Although he is coarse, Chestnut is very discerning. In one
scene (Act III, vv. 449-68), he is dressed in the clothes of
Leonor and in his foolish way he considers himself attractive.
When Don Pedro mistakes him for Leonor and starts to make
love to him, Chestnut determines to get rid of Don Pedro by
being gross:

because you are an unfortunate,
your sister is a mother-in-law,
your maids are aunts,
and your servants beasts. (Act III, vv. 461-64)

But amidst this bold talk he is capable of saying in an aside:

> It's a great thing to be beseeched!
> I no longer wonder why
> women are so proud,
> for nothing makes for pride
> like being beseeched. (Act II, vv. 449-53)

As far as the *gracioso* of Sor Juana is concerned, love always has a strong mercenary character:

> CHESTNUT
> Señor, the greatest sorrow
> love can offend us with
> is to love a kitchen maid
> and have nothing for a gift;
> for if I fall in love
> I am confused, ashamed,
> since I cannot make her love me
> with no money to my name. (Act II, vv. 485-92)

IV Love

In *The Trials of a Noble House* Sor Juana develops certain themes that merit the reader's attention since they are universal in Spanish literature. The dominant theme is love, the various kinds of love, with the companion themes of jealousy and honor (the *pundonor*). Doña Ana describes all the aspects of love at the beginning of Act I (vv. 13-116) when she summarizes the action that took place before the opening of the play and advances the future action. There is unrequited love, which is *cruel love* (v. 43); a bad kind of love that is vile in its lowliness and treatment (v. 53); a rival love, which causes more suffering than the disdain of the woman loved (v. 61); a disappointed love that is an envious poison (v. 66); blind love (v. 71); jealous love (v. 83); and a love that spurs the lover to all kinds of entanglements—this is the *enredo* (vv. 85-116). Love in one guise or another is the principal theme of the play.

A servant may comment on the deceits of love:

> CELIA
> Señora, I am not amazed

> since it is nothing new in love,
> to see the truth dressed up
> in the colors of a lie. (Act I, vv. 117-20)

The Lady Leonor perceives an enigma in her lover since he has both beauty and valor, qualities that are supposed to exclude each other. One speech of Leonor brings to mind Calisto's words in the *Celestina* (c. 1499), although the position of the man and woman is reversed:

> See if with these his noble traits,
> and those others of his I do not mention,
> there would remain in a woman
> modesty's defense. (Act I, vv. 461-64)

In a Spanish drama of the seventeenth century the reader expects to find the theme of pure love *(amor honesto)*, and *The Trials of a Noble House* does not disappoint him:

> LEONOR
> Love grew in both alike
> and wanted our happy union
> to find the chaste nuptial couch
> and so confirm
> the unbreakable tie of Hymen.[3] (Act I, vv. 475-80)

This is the theme that Fray Luis de León (1527-1591) defined in his book *La perfecta casada (The Perfect Wife)*.

Pure love is seen in Act II, vv. 391-97, where Don Carlos does not make a rash judgment of Leonor in spite of appearances that greatly compromise her good name. The theme of pure love also affects the form of the play, and the reader will find expressions used by the Spanish writers of the sixteenth and seventeenth centuries:

> ¿Qué dices, Celia? Primero
> que yo de Don Pedro sea,
> verás de su eterno alcázar
> fugitivas las estrellas;
> primero romperá el mar
> la no violada obediencia
> que a sus desbocadas olas

> *impone freno de arena;*
> *primero aquese fogoso*
> *corazón de las Esferas*
> *perturbará el orden con que*
> *el cuerpo del orbe alienta;*
> *primero, trocado el orden*
> *que guarda Naturaleza,*
> *congelerá el fuego copos,*
> *brotará el hielo centellas;*
> *primero que yo de Carlos,*
> *aunque ingrato me desprecia,*
> *deje de ser, de mi vida*
> *seré verdugo yo mesma;* (Act III, vv. 55-74)

> LEONOR
> What say you, Celia?
> Ere I belong to Don Pedro
> you will see from their eternal keep
> fugitive the stars,
> will see the ocean breach
> the never ravished obedience
> the frame of sands imposes
> on its unbridled waves;
> First that fiery
> heart of Spheres [the sun]
> will upset the order
> by which this earth's body breathes;
> First, the chain undone
> that Nature now insists on,[4]
> a frigid fire will fashion flakes
> and ice will shower sparks;
> I, ere I of Carlos,
> though thankless he doth scorn me,
> cease to be,
> shall turn hangman of myself;

The ordered nature of the Scholastic philosophers will have to turn itself inside out and upside down before this lady will be untrue to her lover.

There is one more kind of love, which was mentioned above in the paragraphs on the *gracioso:* the love of the servants is coarse and mercenary, because it tends toward material things rather than the soul.

V   *Jealousy-Honor* (Celos-Pundonor)

The questions of jealousy and honor arise from the many
conflicting loves in the play and from entanglements *(enredos)*
such as identities mistaken in the dark and conversations over-
heard by people who are frequently hidden in the garden. They
are similar to the questions of jealousy and honor found in other
Spanish plays of the period.

For example, in Act III, vv. 150-52, Don Juan says:

> Would to God
> my jealousy and hurts
> were mere suspicion.

He examines the nature of jealousy and concludes that since his
honor is at stake he can take vengeful action merely on the
grounds of suspicion and presumption. A man does not need
evidence in questions of honor; to have doubted suffices.

There is an interlude in the second act that serves to relieve
the action of the play and also emphasize the themes of love
and jealousy. Amidst a great deal of singing and music, a figure
named Music sings out:

> What is the greatest pain
> that the pains of love contain? (Act II, vv. 413-14)

> Voice I answers:

> To lack favor
> must be the pain
> since it is the greatest ill.
> CHORUS I
> It is not so.
> VOICE I
> It is so.
> CHORUS II
> Well, then, what is? (Act II, vv. 415-20)

Four more voices proceed to answer the question of love's
greatest pain: Voice II, "the sleepless nights for jealousy's de-
light"; Voice III, "the impatience born of absence"; Voice IV,
"anxious care to whoever possesses the beloved"; Voice V, "not

to possess the beloved, when love is freely returned." Chorus II
decides that the last voice, V, has won the competition since its
answer fits the love of Leonor and Carlos, who are kept apart by
the entanglements of the play. After the Choruses and Voices
disappear, all the characters, including the *gracioso* Chestnut,
give their version of "What is the greatest pain/that the pains of
love contain?" This interlude covers the central part of Act II
and unifies the principal themes of the play.

The title of the play, *Los empeños de una casa*, deserves special
attention since it is too much like Calderón's *Los empeños de un
acaso* to be a coincidence. Calderón's play has a jealous father
who is protecting his daughter's honor and a jealous brother who
is protecting his sister's honor, and in both plays the young lady
called Leonor is the daughter of the stern father. By her use of
the title, *Los empeños de una casa,* Sor Juana is stating not only
the source but the spirit of her theater. Within the play's fiction
Chestnut may say he was born in America (Act III, v. 296), but
the historical truth is that he was born in the Spain of Calderón.

VI   *The Second* Sainete

In order to explain the second *sainete* it is necessary to
describe the way *The Trials of a Noble House* was staged. It
was not presented by itself but as part of a *festejo* or festival,
in which there were some ten parts. Before and after the play
and during the intermissions, the actors came forth and recited
verses in honor of the viceroy and his family; they also put on
two *sainetes* or one-act plays (skits). In the second *sainete,*
which appeared between Acts II and III, Sor Juana decided to
provide her audience with some good theatrical fun. She pre-
tends that the author of *The Trials of a Noble House* is a man
called Acevedo (the fact is there was a playwright by that
name).[5]

The second *sainete* begins with a pun based on the word
jornada, which in Spanish can mean either an act of a play,
a day's journey, or simply a journey. A man called Arias is
speaking with his friend Muñiz and he says that the actors have
travelled a long way in the two *jornadas* thus far; if they keep
up they will all arrive at Cavite in the Philippine Islands, where
a good prison cell awaits them. Therefore he invites Muñiz to
sit down with him and gossip about the play.

Muñiz says he has gone through the two acts *(jornadas)* on what seems like a hired mule, and he is so tired he can't even voice a complaint. But finally he agrees and asks:

> Who could it be
> who deceived that poor fellow Deza[6]
> with this old play,
> so great in length and so short on plot?

Arias says the author was a very young writer and such a novice at poetry that "the verses spring forth about as much as the hair on his lip." He says it would have been better to offer a play from Spain, "one by Calderón, Moreto, or Rojas."

Towards the middle of the *sainete* Muñiz asks Arias if there is anything they can do to stop the play, and Arias replies that they can pretend to be *mosqueteros* and destroy the play by hissing (the *mosqueteros* were spectators in the seventeenth-century theater who saw the play on foot from the back of the courtyard; they were very demanding and would hiss a play they did not like). Muñiz heartily agrees, although he himself cannot join in the hissing since he can't pronounce the letter *s*.

Arias hisses, others hiss off stage, and now the real fun and ridicule of the piece begin, for the poor author Acevedo comes forth with the members of his company:

> ACEVEDO
> What hisses are those so atrocious?
> MUNIZ
> That is "so many hisses, so many voices!"
> ACEVEDO
> Do they dare so much the *mosqueteros!*
> ARIAS
> Why, they would hiss the Nava de Zuheros.[7]
> ACEVEDO
> Ay, hissed am I! Ay, unhappy!
> They have hissed my play on me!
> Hisses the first time out? I die.

Acevedo is a ridiculous figure who has come forth to protest the hissing of the *mosqueteros* and Sor Juana has him distort the well-known verse of Segismundo in Calderón's *Life Is a Dream*

(*¡Ay, mísero de mí/Ay infelice!*) into "Ay, hissed am I! Ay, unhappy!"[8]

Acevedo threatens to get out of his difficulty by hanging himself with a rope he has prepared, but they all make fun of him. Then they all hiss in unison. Acevedo says:

> They sound like Spanish boys
> just come over,
> the theater's tumbling down
> with all their hisses.

(This is the second reference to the pronunciation of the Spanish language. Muñiz can't pronounce the letter *s* [many Americans drop their *s*'s], whereas the Spaniards stress their *s* and give a *th* sound to the sibilant *z*.)

Acevedo is bewildered and the other actors sing out:

> Pile on hisses, more!
> Hiss, friends,
> In all that's hollow.
> For hisses do resound.

The poor Acevedo promises never to write another play, but they are not satisfied: this most criminal act of his demands a greater punishment:

> ARIAS
> You must copy down once more
> what you have written.
> ACEVEDO
> Not that, for that
> punishment is so great
> I prefer to die drowned
> in hissing.
> MUNIZ
> He has requested it, he has.
> Hiss, friends,
> For hisses do resound
> In all that's hollow.

Sor Juana has left her audience a good deal of theatrical fun in this short *sainete* (177 verses).

Sor Juana's second *sainete*, owing to the ridiculous mood it creates, is like the two *mojigangas* of Calderón (a *mojiganga* is a brief theatrical piece with ridiculous and outlandish figures; it is designed to cause laughter). In *Los flatos (Flatus)* Calderón brings all the nonsense to an end with singing and dancing:

> Oh you, you gluttonous dame,
> look in this liquid ball,
> see, know, and consider
> that this glass on the outside
> your stomach is on the inside.[9]

In Sor Juana's second *sainete* there are no stage directions for dancing, although dancing could easily be brought into the piece, but there is singing and nonsensical hissing.

In his other *mojiganga*, called *Death*, Calderón presents the laughable scene of a wanderer who stops to rest and meets "The Soul," "The Body," "An Angel," "The Devil," and "Death," all of whom are actors from a nearby playgroup whose cart has overturned in a river. There is a lot of noise and a quick succession of voices. Sor Juana uses this same kind of noise and the theater-within-a-theater in her second *sainete*, where the actors take it upon themselves to play the *mosquetero* and jeer the author. This theater-within-a-theater has been likened to the drama of Pirandello, but the comparison is excessive since the *sainete* hardly has the depth of Pirandello. The joke Sor Juana plays on herself and other persons is autocritical; Pirandello, moreover, raises problems concerning dramatic reality that are absent from Sor Juana's short *sainete*.[10]

VII   Amor es más laberinto (Love, the Greater Labyrinth)

Sor Juana wrote this play in collaboration with the Licenciado Juan de Guevara; she wrote the first and third acts and he wrote the second.

The plot of *Amor es más laberinto (Love, the Greater Labyrinth)* is based on the legend of Theseus and the Minotaur of Crete. The city of Athens, which had incurred the wrath of King Minos of Crete, had to send fourteen of its youth every year to Crete. There they were sacrificed to the Minotaur, the monster with a bull's body and a human head, who devoured

them. The Minotaur lived in a labyrinth that had such a maze
of tunnels, no one who entered it could ever find his way out
even if he destroyed the monster.

Theseus, whose father was King of Athens, resolved to go to
Crete as one of the fourteen victims in order to have a chance of
destroying the monster. When he got to Crete he was brought
before King Minos, whose daughter Ariadne fell in love with
him when she saw him. She provided him a sword with which to
fight the Minotaur, and a thread to unravel so that he could find
his way out of the labyrinth. Theseus was successful in destroying
the Minotaur and in emerging from the maze of tunnels alive.
He later sailed for Athens and took Ariadne with him, but he
abandoned her on the island of Naxos. When Theseus got back
to Athens, he found that his father was dead and he was King.

Love, The Greater Labyrinth

Act I

In the play Sor Juana has added several characters to those
mentioned above. The cast of characters is the following:

Minos, King of Crete	Lidorus, Prince of Epirus
Ariadne, his daughter	An ambassador from Athens
Phaedra, his daughter	Tebandrus, Captain of the Guard
Theseus, Prince of Athens	Laura, Phaedra's servant
Tunafish, his servant	Cynthia, Ariadne's servant
(a *gracioso*)	
Bacchus, Prince of Thebes	Licas, Athenian general
Clusterbunch, his servant	Athenian soldiers
(a *gracioso*)	

In the first act the characters talk about the famous labyrinth.
Theseus has arrived in Crete, the day before the opening scene
of the play, and soon he is to be sacrificed to the Minotaur.

Theseus appears before King Minos and in a long speech
(vv. 423-700) describes his famous deeds. He cuts such a figure
that both Ariadne and Phaedra fall in love with him. Although
he himself falls in love with Phaedra, Ariadne determines to
save him by giving him a thread so that he can extricate himself
from the labyrinth.

In the first act there are several love entanglements *(enredos)*
involving the two princes, Lidorus and Bacchus.

Act II

The Captain of the Guard explains to King Minos that he has already delivered Theseus to the Minotaur. They talk about the labyrinth and then the captain says that the princesses have prepared a masked ball *(sarao)* for the entertainment of Minos. The King says he will go to the ball in an effort to assuage his wrath.

After the captain and the King go off, Theseus and Tunafish come out of the labyrinth; Theseus has killed the monster. Tunafish tells him about the *sarao* and how everyone will be disguised there. Theseus, whose survival is unknown to the King, decides to go to the *sarao*, where he is to wear a ribbon that will enable his true love, Phaedra, to recognize him. Meanwhile, Ariadne's servant gives him a feather that he is to wear so that Ariadne will recognize him. All the entanglements of the second act now begin, for the feather, which Theseus gives to Tunafish, falls into the hands of Prince Bacchus; in the darkness of the night, moreover, Theseus whispers words of love to Ariadne, whom he takes to be Phaedra. The confusion mounts, since all the masked characters mistake one another's identity in the dark.

Act III

The servant Clusterbunch carries a letter from Bacchus to Lidorus. Owing to the confusion of the *sarao*, Bacchus wishes to challenge the other prince to a duel. The letter falls into Theseus' hands, the King orders Bacchus to go off with him to fight the Athenian fleet that is nearing Crete, and Theseus fights with Lidorus and kills him. This duel underlies the entanglements of the third act, since many believe that Bacchus has killed Lidorus, whereas Theseus himself thinks he has killed Bacchus.

The confusion grows in the third act until some three hundred verses before the end of the play. The Athenians have captured Crete and they now turn over the civil and military power to Theseus.

Theseus pardons the life of King Minos. Tunafish recites some verses reviewing the action and *enredos* of the third act. Then Theseus says that he will marry Phaedra, and Bacchus says he will marry Ariadne. The two ladies accept their proposal.

VIII   *The Three Labyrinths*

In the legend of Theseus and the Minotaur of Crete, there
is one labyrinth: the maze of tunnels where the monster dwells
and fourteen youths are sacrificed every year. There is also one
thread: the piece of yarn that Ariadne gives Theseus so he can
find his way out of the tunnels; this thread disentangles, that
is, it clears up a puzzle. In *Love, the Greater Labyrinth,* however, there are three labyrinths and a thread that becomes a
maze of threads.

The first labyrinth is the same as the one in the legend, namely,
the maze where the Minotaur is confined, where Athens must
send fourteen young people each year to satisfy the vengeance
of Minos, who lost his son at Athenian hands. This labyrinth is
explained early in the play by Phaedra's servant Laura (Act I,
vv. 74-124) and by the King (Act I, vv. 203-70). It also has a
companion image, the thread *(hilo).* Every labyrinth has some
kind of solution: the valor of Theseus and the thread Ariadne
gives him so that he can extricate himself from the passageways
and overcome the maze where the Minotaur is kept. There is
never any doubt of Theseus' ability to conquer the monster; the
only problematical thing is the labyrinth:

ARIADNE
I can free him since I have
a cunning stratagem.
Though Phaedra may be his love
my love will not permit
that for me,
if I adore him, he be unhappy.
CYNTHIA
By what means can you free him?
ARIADNE
They are subtle,
for with one thread alone
he shall triumph;
since in battle
he will know how to vanquish the proud monster.
(I, vv. 1039-50)

Ariadne's words concern the first labyrinth, where the Minotaur
dwells, but they also touch on the third and most important
labyrinth, the labyrinth of love. Love also has a subtle thread,

or rather it has many threads that serve to entangle the lover rather than liberate him.

The second labyrinth is the form of the play itself: the maze of entanglements, mistaken identities, eavesdroppings, and masked characters. This labyrinth is the weakest part of the play, because the idea that love is a greater entanglement than the fabulous passageways of Crete with their monstrous Minotaur is a transcendent theme that does not fit into the stock actions of this *comedia de enredo*.

The third labyrinth is the principal theme and title of the play, *Love, the Greater Labyrinth*. The labyrinth of Crete has a maze of tunnels with one monster at the center and one thread for the extrication of a man such as Theseus; but the labyrinth of Love is a maze with many monsters—jealousy, suspicion, doubt, mistakes, unrequited affection—and the thread that a lover gives a man becomes many threads rather than one, and rather than extricate him from the maze, it ensnares and puzzles him all the more. Thus Love is the great labyrinth, greater even than the fabulous maze of Crete.

IX *Theseus' Speech*

In Act I Theseus has a long speech that is interesting for the ideas it contains.

In the socio-political part of the speech Theseus tells the King he prides himself more on being a good soldier than on being a prince. A good soldier may become a prince but a prince without valor can never acquire it. He illustrates how a valorous man can acquire a kingdom. He argues that men once lived in absolute equality in a state of nature; nothing distinguished one man from another except deeds and since no man would forfeit his liberty and equality voluntarily, for man is born with the natural tendency to rule, it follows that some men of great deeds must have forcefully introduced the inequality we now see between king and vassal, noble and plebeian; only force can explain why some serve today as slaves whereas others rule as lords.[11]

Then Theseus starts to recount his deeds. When he comes to his fight with the Amazons, he brings in the theme of woman:

> In whose company [Hercules] I achieved
> midst many other trophies.

> a victory of the Amazons:
> And not without cause I call
> this the greatest of my triumphs,
> sir, for I believe
> the conquering of a woman
> the greatest of all victories:
> for how to overcome
> an enemy who both
> captivates through sight
> and fights with steel?
> And if she is not comely
> her womanliness doth suffice,
> a great advantage:
> for in addition to her strength
> there fight for her
> my feeling and respect. (Act I, vv. 537-54)

These lines about the Amazons deserve mention since their courtly nature is a key to this play and to the secular literature of Sor Juana. She was the poetess of a seventeenth-century Spanish court.

As Theseus talks about his deeds, he says he is an instrument of justice who has destroyed cruel men and tyrants. When he comes to his triumph over the Centaurs, who tried to carry off the wife of his friend Piritus, he says he does not seek praise: because he who is my true friend is I, I myself, and not another I, and if he is offended I am offended and so in righting the wrong I do it for myself and act out of jealous interest rather than courage (Act I, vv. 632-46).

This idea that a person's friend is he himself might have come from Montaigne's essay on his friendship with Etienne La Boetie, although a more probable source is Cicero.[12]

When Theseus said he considered his victory over the Amazons his greatest triumph, he was saying in effect that his greatest victory was the one he gained over himself. Such a statement was a common thought in Sor Juana's day. Furthermore, when Helen with all her beauty was at his mercy, not only did Theseus not force himself on her, he listened to her pleas and returned her to her country, leaving his own love for her in tears:

> my love for her went weeping,
> and my courage achieved

that victory most dear:
to conquer mine own self. (Act I, vv. 673-76)

Theseus ends his speech saying he will die content if his death
will spare the future victims of the Minotaur.

Shortly after Theseus' speech, the play becomes a *comedia
de enredo* rather than a mythological play or a play with the
transcendental theme of love as a labyrinth: Ariadne eavesdrops
(v. 825); Bacchus eavesdrops (v. 1051); Bacchus makes a mistake in identity (v. 1096); Bacchus will feign love for Phaedra
in order to get back at his supposed rival Lidorus, who is not
really his rival (v. 1137)—and so on.

X *A Criticism of the Play*

In spite of its use of the legend of Theseus and the Minotaur,
Love, the Greater Labyrinth is not so much a mythological play
as a *comedia de enredo* similar to *The Trials of a Noble House*.
The mistaken identities and other entanglements of Theseus,
Bacchus, Phaedra, and Ariadne are cut of the same cloth as the
entanglements of Pedro, Carlos, Ana, and Leonor. In the case of
Love, the Greater Labyrinth, the innumerable *enredos* detract
from the play, because the idea that love is a greater entanglement than the fabulous passageways of Crete with their monstrous Minotaur is a transcendent theme that does not fit into the
stock actions of this *comedia de enredo*.

Love, the Greater Labyrinth should have been written in the
fashion of Lope de Vega's *Peribáñez*, Calderón's *The Mayor of
Zalamea*, or Rojas Zorrilla's *None Except the King*. The play
should have the Labyrinth of Crete with its one Minotaur and one
thread, and the *Labyrinth of Love* with its several minotaurs and
several threads. In such a play Theseus would not experience
much difficulty with the Cretan labyrinth and Minotaur; the
other threads and Minotaurs, however, coming as they would
from within a man's breast, from the pangs of jealousy, from the
honor of a woman, from the problem of what course of action to
take, and from a Minotaur personified in an evil knight com-
mander, captain or count—these threads and minotaurs would
make a great deal of dramatic action. To sum up, there is a
disparity between the *comedia de enredo* and the theme of love
as a great labyrinth.

As for the *gracioso*, Tunafish (Atún) and Clusterbunch
(Racimo) meet several times in the play, and it must be said
that the humor based on their names and on the relation of
Bacchus to Clusterbunch is overdone. (Bacchus is the Greek
god of wine and *racimo* is the Spanish word for a cluster of
grapes.)

It is possible that Sor Juana found a suggestion for *Love, the
Greater Labyrinth* in Lope de Vega's *Labyrinth of Crete* and
in Cervantes' *The Labyrinth of Love,* but neither of these can
be considered the source of her play. Lope's *comedia* (he himself
called it a tragedy) sticks much closer to the legend; for example,
the ungrateful Theseus abandons Ariadne on an island and carries
off Phaedra in his arms. Lope's servant is also quite different:
Fineo has such a high sense of honor that he rebukes Theseus
for abandoning his saviour Ariadne and elects to stay on the
island with her. There may be a faint resemblance to Sor Juana's
play in Lope's escape scene, in which Theseus and Fineo leave
with the two ladies for the sea, but there is no basic likeness
between Lope's mythological play and Sor Juana's *comedia de
enredo.*[13]

As for Cervantes, his play seems to be the opposite of Sor
Juana's. There are a great many entanglements (unknown identities, ladies dressed as men, masked men, false accusations) in
Cervantes' play, but in spite of the fact that these continue until
the end, they always have a subordinate position: the action of
the play is made to serve the theme of love as a labyrinth. The
theme is always uppermost and when, for example, Julia comes
and kneels before Manfredo to tell him that she herself was the
boy called Camilo who told Manfredo of Julia's love, the play
acquires a strange beauty that is peculiar to the art of Cervantes.
In Sor Juana's play, on the other hand, the theme of love is
subordinate to the complicated plot.

XI *The Other Parts of* The Festival
of The Trials of a Noble House

The *loa,* the first *sainete,* the three *letras* and the *sarao* of
The Festival of The Trials of a Noble House do not have the
literary value of the play itself and the second *sainete.* However,
they give us an insight into the social and intellectual history
of Sor Juana's day and so we shall discuss them briefly here.

The *loa* that precedes the first act of the play is a contest between the four abstract figures, Merit, Diligence, Fortune, and Chance. The question proposed to them is twofold: (1) What is the greatest of all joys? and (2) Through which of these four abstract figures is this joy most easily arrived at? In the logomachy that follows, Diligence allies herself with Merit (masculine), and Chance allies himself with Fortune (feminine). Merit asks Fortune several scornful questions, for example: "Are you not of discord/ an ill-governed clock?" And Fortune replies by listing all of her conquests in history. These conquests of Alexander, Tamerlane, Caesar, Theseus, and Ulysses have a certain dramatic quality that is found frequently in Sor Juana, even in her nondramatic poetry.

The contest continues, and the four figures keep advancing their ingenious arguments. In the growing confusion, the lady Music, to whom they appeal, first agrees with and then disagrees with all of them. Finally they invoke Joy herself, who settles the problem by saying that all four can attain to ordinary joys but that she herself is not ordinary. Joy defines herself as

> the happy arrival
> of the sublime María
> and Invincible Cerda,
> may they live happy and long endure. (Verses 404-7)

That is, Joy came with the happy arrival of the Viceroy (Don Tomás Antonio de la Cerda) and his wife, María.

This *loa*, which generally imitates the style of the *auto sacramental*, does not make for very good theater. The dramatic action between the abstract figures is forced, most of the verses are wooden, and the last hundred-odd verses are a mechanical tribute to the new rulers of Mexico.

The Three Letras

In *The Festival* there are three poems, *letras*, placed before and after the first and second acts of the play. These *letras* were written for the Viceroy's wife and her son. Like the *loa* before them, they lack poetic inspiration.

The First Sainete

The first *sainete* is a contest *(certamen)* that is similar to the *loa*, although it is less than half as long (the *loa*, 535 verses;

this *sainete*, 202 verses). The judge of the contest is the Alcalde del Terrero, the presiding officer of the area in the palace where the gentlemen woo the ladies, and it is he who gets things going by calling forth the five logical beings, Love, Respect, Courtesy, Kindness, and Hope. All of them must vie for the prize, which is the scorn of the ladies: "Scorn is here the prize,/and even that costs pain."

Since the figures are abstract, and since the prize is unusual in that it is negative, this contest of courtly love leans heavily on ingenious reasons. Love does not merit the prize because he is a courtesy and not a contract; Courtesy does not win because the very fact that the ladies let him serve them is his reward. The Alcalde concludes:

> Let them know then,
> those who serve at Court,
> that even scorn itself
> is beyond their reach.

This first *sainete* may hold some interest for the social historian, but it is too contrived and abstract to be considered good theater.

The Sarao *of the Four Nations*

There are four nations—Spaniards, Negroes, Italians, and Mexicans—who come to pay homage to the Viceroy and his family. The first chorus of Negroes sings:

> *Hoy, que los rayos lucientes*
> *de uno y otro luminar,*
> *a corta Esfera conmutan*
> *la Eclíptica celestial;*
> *hoy, que Venus con Adonis,*
> *ésta bella, aquél galán,*
> *a breve plantel reducen*
> *de Chipre la amenidad.* (vv. 70-77)

> Today, since the rays of light
> of one luminary and another,
> bring to this poor Sphere
> the heavenly Ecliptic;
> today, when Venus with Adonis,
> she beautiful, he most gallant,
> enclose in this humble nursery
> the amenity of Cyprus;

It is unfortunate that Sor Juana was so imposed upon she had to put these dull incongruities into the mouths of the Negroes of 1683, because she had a real gift for the theatrical; and for her Carols (*Villancicos*) of the Feast of the Assumption, 1676, she had written the following words for the Negroes of Carol VIII:

> -¡Ah, ah, ah,
> que la Reina se nos va!
> -¡Uh, uh, uh,
> que non blanca como tú,
> nin Pañó que no sa buena,
> que Eya dici: So molena
> con las Sole que mirá!
> -¡Ah, ah, ah,
> que la Reina se nos va!

> Ah, ah, ah,
> oh the Queen she goes away!
> Uh, uh, uh,
> she is not white a like a you,
> nor a Spanish which is not good,
> cause she says: I am brown
> from the Sun what smiled on me!
> Ah, ah, ah,
> oh the Queen she goes away!

CHAPTER 4

The Religious Theater

THE religious theater of Sor Juana consists of three *autos sacramentales* or sacramental plays, three *loas* or preludes to these sacramental plays, and a *loa* praising the Immaculate Conception. The sacramental play called *El divino Narciso (The Divine Narcissus)*, which is partially based on the myth of Echo and Narcissus, is Sor Juana's masterpiece.

I The Myth of Echo and Narcissus

Echo was a beautiful nymph who was extremely fond of talking. She incurred the wrath of Juno and this great goddess punished her by taking away her power of speech, except for one thing: in speaking to someone Echo could reply using the same words as the other person.

Narcissus was a beautiful youth who disdained all the nymphs that fell in love with him. One of these nymphs was Echo, and when he spoke to her she could only repeat whatever he said.

One day an avenging goddess (Nemesis) decided to punish Narcissus by having him suffer the same disdain that he showed others. Narcissus came to a fountain with a clear pool of water in which he saw his own image. He fell in love with his image, but every time he approached it, it disappeared—it disdained him. He now knew the hurt that Echo had felt and, like her, he pined away and passed into nothingness. Echo's voice alone remains, in the high mountain tops, and the only trace of Narcissus, whose body was never found, is the flower that bears his name.

II El divino Narciso (The Divine Narcissus)

Cast of Characters

The Divine Narcissus	Echo
Human Nature	Pride
Grace	Self Love
Gentilism	Nymphs and Shepherds
Synagogue	

Two Choruses of Music

In this cast of allegorical characters, the divine Narcissus is Christ; Human Nature is a woman (mankind) who is searching for her lover, Narcissus; Grace, who is the grace of God that leads mankind to Christ, is a friend of Human Nature; Gentilism represents pagan antiquity; Synagogue represents divine revelation in the Old Testament; Echo represents fallen angelic nature, that is, she is the devil; and Pride and Self Love are allies of Echo. These characters are very human. The allegory never strips them of their humanity, and the blending of mythology and theology is done with taste.

After a heated argument, Synagogue and Gentilism agree that they will stage a sacramental play in which Synagogue will provide the truths of revelation and Gentilism will provide the beauty of pagan antiquity. Together they should make quite a pair.

At this point Human Nature comes forth and, in a long speech, discloses to the audience the meaning of the play's allegory. She herself (mankind) was made in God's image, but the image has been so muddied by the waters of sin that the beautiful Narcissus (Christ) would not recognize Himself if He looked into it; and so Human Nature is looking for some fountain whose waters will cleanse her and enable her to reflect once more the image she was created with. Human Nature can be very moving. She sounds at times like a hurt woman who would like to be forgiven by her lover, Narcissus; in speaking to Synagogue and Gentilism about their sacramental play, she says:

> you, to soften
> the rigor of Narcissus
> repeat His praise

in tender acclamation,
joining tears to your words,
that he might listen.
Tell Him of my grief
since your voice in union
may summon His compassion
and mercy for my pardon. (vv. 257-66)

Echo then appears. Since she is a woman who represents fallen
angelic nature (the devil), she is naturally accompanied by the
shepherdess Pride and the shepherd Self Love. This departure
from the letter of ancient mythology makes possible the dramatic
conflict in which Echo and her friends struggle with the divine
Narcissus for the destiny of the lady Human Nature (mankind).
Echo and her friends are upset because they have heard har-
monious voices singing in the forest, praising the Lord and
Narcissus; it is the harmony that bothers these princes of discord.

Echo has a long speech (vv. 295-526) in which she does
something that one figure or another always does in the sacramental plays: she explains who she is and then she recounts the
prominent episodes of the Old Testament.

Because of her intuitive knowledge(v. 296), Echo knows that
Human Nature (mankind) is seeking Beauty itself (God) even
though Beauty has scorned her. Echo says that she has "dragged
the third part of the Angels from the Stars to the Abyss," which
is a reference to the rebellion of Lucifer, and then she mentions
her own beauty in a striking way:

You must know that I am Echo,
she of discontented beauty,
who since she would be more fair
came less so and more ungainly, (vv. 373-76)

The joint appearance of unhappiness and beauty is found again in
vv. 775-78, in the scene where Echo tempts Narcissus:

I am Echo, the richest girl,
shepherdess of all these valleys;
my great beauty can be described
in my wretchedness, my malady.

This is a common theme in the literature of the time, which the reader will also meet in Sor Juana's play *The Trials of a Noble House:* Leonor is beautiful; then she must be unhappy (beautiful women are unhappy since many would soil their beauty). In the diabolical Echo, however, the theme has an unusually profound application. The archangel Lucifer was by nature the most beautiful creature of God's Creation, the most God-like, and so he aspired to the union of his nature with God's. When his hopes were disappointed he turned into a proud rebel, and the exile that followed caused this most beautiful of creatures to be the most unhappy. But listen to the woman Echo (the devil):

> *porque—viéndome dotada*
> *de hermosura y de nobleza,*
> *de valor y de virtud,*
> *de perfección y de ciencia,*
> *y en fin, viendo que era yo,*
> *aun de la Naturaleza*
> *Angélica ilustre mía,*
> *la criatura más perfecta—*
> *ser esposa de Narciso*
> *quise, e intenté soberbia*
> *poner mi asiento en Su Solio*
> *e igualarme a su grandeza,*
> *juzgando que no*
> *era inconsecuencia*
> *que fuera igual Suya*
> *quien era tan bella;*
> *por lo cual, El, ofendido,*
> *tan desdeñoso me deja,*
> *tan colérico me arroja*
> *de Su gracia y Su presencia,*
> *que no me dejó ¡ay de mí!*
> *esperanza de que pueda*
> *volver a gozar los rayos*
> *de Su Divina Belleza.* (vv. 377-400)

> for—seeing I had the gift
> of nobility and beauty
> and also courage and power,
> of perfection and of knowledge,
> and in short seeing that I was
> even of Angelic Nature

the most illustrious boast—
I willed to marry Narcissus,
and I attempted in my pride
to place myself upon His throne
to equal Him in His grandeur,
and I judged there was no discord
that I in my peerless beauty
should rival Him in grace;
due to which He was offended,
so disdainful has He left me
so wrathful has He exiled me
from His joy as from His presence
that I have not, to my sorrow,
the hope that I'll enjoy again
the rays of His divine Beauty.[1]

Echo (the devil) is afraid that Human Nature (mankind) will acquire the laurels she herself has lost. She caused Human Nature to offend the infinite Narcissus by original sin, because she reasoned that an infinite offense would require infinite atonement, which Human Nature of course could never give. Echo's one remaining task is to keep Narcissus (Christ) from looking into Human Nature's eyes lest He fall in love with that lowly village maid:

a vile town girl,
formed of rustic clay
and struck from lowly matter. (vv. 448-50)

Echo has explained who she is, and now she emphasizes the episodes of the Old Testament that have captured the imagination: the Deluge, Noah's Ark, and the Tower of Babel. The Deluge has a special importance in *The Divine Narcissus* since it pertains to the most significant image of the play, water. The sins of Human Nature are turbulent waters:

And so it is well I name
my sin muddy waters,
whose obscene hue
stand between Him and me. (vv. 232-35)

Human Nature seeks the cleansing waters of baptism:

let us seek the Fountain
in which my stains will be washed away (vv. 269-71)

But the most puissant water is the Fountain through which all
grace must pass, the Virgin Mary:

> HUMAN NATURE
> And what then must I do?
> GRACE
> You must follow me
> and come to that Fountain
> whose crystal waters,
> free of sullied fluid,
> always pure, intact
> from their first moment
> have ever flowed without stain.
> That is the Sealed Fountain
> in the Song of Songs
> which springs forth from Paradise
> rich in living water. (vv. 1114-24)

The Divine Narcissus has looked into many waters and failed to
see His countenance, but when He looks into this one immaculate
fountain He sees Himself purely reflected there and falls in love
with His image, that is, with Human Nature (vv. 1326-95). The
transition from legend to theology is charming.

Echo's long speech ends on the note of idolatry: men in their
ignorance so adored statues they were almost transformed into
them, although there have always been a few to remind man of
his divine origin.

After Echo's long speech, Sor Juana brings some spectacle and
singing into the play, which provide relief for the audience and
prepare it for the main action that is soon to come. The stage
directions read: "The second cart [the sacramental plays were
staged on several carts[2]] is opened; and Abel, on high, begins
to move about and lights the fire; and he conceals himself, while
singing: . . ."; "Enoch passes in the same way, on his knees, his
hands folded in prayer, and he sings: . . ."; "Then Abraham
comes, as they picture him [sacrificing his son], and the Angel
sings: . . . ."; "Moses passes by with the Tablets of the Law, and
he sings: . . ." (see vv. 538-73).

The spectacle of Abel, Enoch, Abraham, and Moses is followed by two of the most memorable scenes of the play: Christ's temptation by the devil, and Human Nature's search for God in the manner of St. John of the Cross. Both of these scenes have an extraordinary human quality. The art of Sor Juana is not lost in her Christian message—she is not guilty of preaching.

Narcissus has been fasting for forty days when the devil comes to tempt Him in the form of the woman Echo:

> And so I intend to come
> amorous and attractive;
> for who will deny the lure's strength
> if in woman's guise it is proffered? (vv. 685-90)

Echo tells Narcissus she is the richest shepherdess of all these valleys and starts to flatter Him as a woman will a man. She shows Him her wealth:

> You may cast Your eyes where You will
> from this lofty peak that puts shame
> to the glory of Mount Atlas.
> See those herds, see
> how flooding all the valleys
> they graze upon the emeralds
> offered by the fruitful plains. (vv. 747-54)

Echo (the devil) keeps describing her wealth, and then as a woman she tempts Narcissus:

> All this, fair Narcissus,
> is subject to my law
> and my possession;
> it is my gift and dowry.
> Which soon shall be Yours
> if you with gracious mien
> cast off Your rigid shell
> and come now to adore me. (vv. 795-802)

This temptation of Christ is a very human one.

After Echo fails in her enticement, the scene changes to a landscape of field and forest, with a fountain in the background. Human Nature appears and in the style of the Song of Songs

and the poetry of St. John of the Cross she tells of her distress
and longing:

> *De buscar a Narciso fatigada,*
> *sin permitir sosiego a mi pie errante,*
> *ni a mi planta cansada*
> *que tantos ha ya días que vagante*
> *examina las breñas*
> *sin poder encontrar más que las señas,*
> *a este bosque he llegado donde espero*
> *tener noticias de mi Bien perdido;*
> *que si señas confiero,*
> *diciendo está del prado lo florido,*
> *que producir amenidades tantas,*
> *es por haber besado ya Sus plantas.* (vv. 819-30)

> Weary I look for Narcissus,
> take no ease in my errant journey,
> nor grant it to my feet
> which many days grow lame
> probing in the thickets
> to find no more of Him than traces.
> I come to this forest where I hope
> to learn news of my Good whom I have lost;
> and I shall if I watch the signs,
> like this meadow steeped in flowers,
> which owing to its great delight
> he surely caressed as He travelled.

> *¡Oh ninfas que habitáis este florido*
> *y ameno prado, ansiosamente os ruego*
> *que si acaso al Querido*
> *de mi alma encontraréis, de mi fuego*
> *Le noticiéis, diciendo el agonía*
> *con que de amor enferma el alma mía!*
> *Si queréis que os dé señas de mi Amado,*
> *rubicundo esplendor Le colorea*
> *sobre jazmín nevado;*
> *por su cuello, rizado Ofir pasea;*
> *los ojos, de paloma que enamora*
> *y en los raudales transparentes mora.* (vv. 849-60)

> Oh nymphs who dwell in this meadow,
> oh you who dwell in these flowers,

anxiously I pray
if you see my soul's Beloved you will say
that I burn from fire and suffer pain
for love that sears my soul with endless flame
If you would know the face of my Beloved
a reddish crown on jazmine is His hue,
and locks of Ophir's gold pass 'round His neck,
His eyes are of a dove that hearts inflames
and abides by rushing waters.

In her long soliloquy (vv. 819-1046) Human Nature shows all
the signs of a woman who is longing for her lover.

Her words, moreover, contain a certain thrill that is found in
all the sacramental plays: it is precisely this thrill that the drama
of these plays is based on. Human Nature (mankind) is very
miserable in this world and must contend with the world's
powerful lord, Echo (the devil). Since man's nature is bent, this
conflict is one-sided and would result in black despair if man
were not able to call upon his Champion, the divine Narcissus
(Christ). He is hard to find, but He always comes and defies
man's enemies (Pride, Self Love, Echo) and He lays down His
life for His friend. If there is one virtue the sacramental plays
extol it is Hope, and if there is one feeling they create it is
confidence, the thrill of being redeemed. The sacramental play is
the supreme artistic recognition of the truth that human life
was meant to be a comedy.

After her soliloquy about her Beloved, Human Nature meets
the shepherdess, Grace, who is singing: "Glad tidings, world, I
bring." The lonely woman believes she has seen the shepherdess
before, which Grace confirms by telling her about a garden where
they were once well acquainted (she is referring, of course, to
the Garden of Eden). Their conversation foretells a great future
event, which will reunite them, and it describes a fountain (the
Blessed Virgin) whose waters have never known poison and so
will serve as the mirror which Narcissus can look into to see His
countenance; they point to the fountain in the background of the
scenery. The shepherdess Grace, who represents divine grace,
concludes by telling Human Nature that since she is with her,
Narcissus (Christ) will definitely come, which he does in the
next scene, the most beautiful of the play.

As Narcissus arrives, Grace and Human Nature hide in the branches near the fountain:

NARCISSUS
[he sings every fifth verse]
Ovejuela perdida,
de tu Dueño olvidada,
¿adónde vas errada:
Mira que dividida
de Mí, también te apartas de tu vida.
Por las cisternas viejas
bebiendo turbias aguas,
tu necia sed enjaguas;
y con sordas orejas,
de las aguas vivíficas te alejas.
En Mis finezas piensa:
verás que, siempre amante,
te guardo vigilante,
te libro de la ofensa,
y que pongo la vida en tu defensa.
De la escarcha y la nieve
cubierto, voy siguiendo
tus necios pasos, viendo
que ingrata no te mueve
ver que dejo por ti noventa y nueve. (vv. 1221-40)

Lost lamb
forgetful of your master
where have you strayed?
See how apart
from me, you are also apart from your life.
By old wells
drinking muddied waters
you slake your foolish thirst
and with deaf ears
you take yourself off from the waters of life.
Think of my gifts
and see that always loving
I watch over you;
I free you of your offense
and I offer up my life for your defense.
Covered with frost and snow
I keep following

your foolish steps and see
ungrateful you are not moved
when I leave the ninety-nine for you, but one.

The Champion, the divine Narcissus, has come to save His people.
Surely the audience is a part of this play.

After singing his last verse (v. 1325), Narcissus goes to the
fountain (the Blessed Virgin) to quench His thirst and He is
amazed and astonished by the great beauty there. At last Narcissus has seen His own image. He falls so much in love with it
that He will die for it.

While Narcissus is entirely absorbed by the fountain, Echo
comes and realizes that He has fallen in love with His image,
which is also the image of Human Nature. Her rage is so great
she feels "an asp, a choking in her throat," which so damages her
speech she can only articulate last words. The Echo of Sor Juana
has become the Echo of mythology:

> PRIDE
> Hold on there, since you I have.
> ECHO
> I have.
> SELF LOVE
> Tell us your burning pain.
> ECHO
> Pain.
> PRIDE
> Tell the cause of your rage.
> ECHO
> Rage.
> SELF LOVE
> Since you are so wise
> Tell us what is the matter,
> what you feel.
> ECHO
> I Have, Pain, Rage.

This peculiar use of the verses known as echoes (*ecos*, in Spanish)
fits in with the meaning of the play and preserves one of the
basic features of the myth; furthermore, the devil is often
referred to as being mute:

since Sacred Letters, which defame me
now and then name me mute.[3] (vv. 1426-27)

The long series of *ecos* is terminated by a sonnet in which
Narcissus commends His Spirit into the hands of His Father
(v. 1705). Then the earth quakes.[4]

The last five hundred verses, which constitute the Eucharistic
argument of this play, have some touching poetry. Human Nature
is disconsolate over the death of her lover, the beautiful Narcissus, and she recites a series of verses called *endechas,* which
end with the refrain "feel, feel my longing,/ mourn, mourn His
death."

As for the Eucharistic argument, Echo plans to attack Human
Nature on the principle that absence makes a person forget:
out of sight, out of mind. Unless Human Nature is constantly
reminded of Narcissus, He will soon vanish from her memory and
Echo (the devil) will have no trouble in dominating her.

> HUMAN NATURE
> Ay, my beloved groom,
> let me but joyfully come
> to kiss your feet.
> NARCISSUS
> You may not touch me
> for I go with My Father
> to His celestial throne.
> HUMAN NATURE
> Then you leave me alone?
> ay, Lord, do not leave me,
> for my enemy the serpent
> will come to harm me. (vv. 1959-68)

Echo is pleased at the news of Narcissus' departure since her
intuitive knowledge (the devil is an angel and has intuitive
knowledge), as great as it is, cannot understand how Narcissus
is able to go away from His bride and nevertheless remain with
her.

In a long speech summing up the Fall and Redemption, Grace
explains that Narcissus has chosen to remain on earth in the
form of a white flower, the Eucharist; thus his absence will not
cause Human Nature to grow lukewarm. Once again Sor Juana

makes a striking comparison between pagan mythology and
Christian doctrine: Narcissus looking into the water—Christ seeking His image in human nature; Narcissus becoming the flower
that bears his name—Christ's presence in the white flower, the
host.

After Grace's speech, Sor Juana quickly does three things that
give unity to the play: (1) the stage directions say: "The cart
with the fountain comes forth, and next to the fountain there is
a chalice with a host above it." This fountain [the Blessed Virgin]
was the scene of the central part of the play (vv. 819-1705). The
chalice and the host are a customary spectacle at the end of a
sacramental play. (2) Echo says: "And I, alas, who have seen
it,/ shall keep mute, shall live/ for sorrow, dead to all alleviation"
(vv. 2196-98). Echo's words remind the audience of her muteness
at the time she recited the *ecos* (vv. 1480-1691). (3) In verse
2220, Grace and Human Nature embrace, an action that was
foretold back in verses 1095-1102, when Human Nature wished
to take Grace in her arms but was refused until "a great event"
should take place, namely, the death of Narcissus.

The play concludes with verses based on the *Gloria Patri* and
the Nicene Creed:

> May glory, honor, benediction and praise
> greatness and power to the Father and Son
> be given; and to the Love that from both proceeds
> may we also bowing down give praise. (vv. 2235-38)

III *The* auto sacramental *and the* loa

An *auto sacramental* is a sacramental play that takes place in
one long act (the word *auto* means *acto,* or in English, "act");
it is roughly two-thirds the length of a three-act *comedia* such as
The Trials of a Noble House. The characters of the sacramental
play are allegorical, and its story is based on some doctrine concerning the Holy Eucharist. The master of the sacramental plays
was Calderón, who wrote them for the Feast of Corpus Christi.

At the beginning of *The Divine Narcissus,* Human Nature says
that she belongs to both Synagogue and Gentilism (Jews and
pagans, in spite of their many differences, both partake of the
same human nature). Then she says she will construct a sacramental play using the revelation of Synagogue and the mythology

of Gentilism; as she says this she explains the allegorical character
of the sacramental plays:

> And thus I since Mother of both I am
> shall try with allegorical color,
> which puts forth representable ideas,
> to take from one the purport and the sense
> to take the charmed language from the other
> so that in fine sentence and metaphor,
> taking their mode of speech, in Narcissus
> I shall beseech the greater love of God
> to see if these dark fumblings and splotches
> can conjure up the brilliance of His light. (vv. 112-24)

The sacramental plays are allegories that use charmed language
to conjure up God's love and light.

The word *loa* is a cognate of the English word "laud," praise.
In the theater a *loa* is a brief dramatic work that may do one
of three things: (1) it may serve as a prelude to a play and
explain to the audience the argument of the work it is about to
see; (2) it may solicit the goodwill of the audience; (3) it may
sing the praises of the dignitary to whom the play is dedicated—
or, it may do all three, serve as a prelude, solicit goodwill, and
praise a famous person. The *loa* had been widely used in the
secular theater, but Calderón used it to introduce the sacramental
plays he wrote for the Feast of Corpus Christi; the *loa of*
Calderón has the same allegorical character as his sacramental
plays. Sor Juana's plays and *loas* belong to the school of Calderón.

IV *The Influence of Calderón*

The reader has seen the similarities between Sor Juana's secular
theater and the theater of Calderón. Her religious theater is also
dependent on the Spanish master, who is considered to be the
foremost writer of sacramental plays.

In her long speech (vv. 295-526). Sor Juana's Echo does
something that one figure or another always does in the sacramental plays of Calderón. She explains who she is and then she
runs the gamut of prominent episodes in the Old Testament. The
theatrical reason for this self-definition and retelling of biblical
history seems to be fourfold: (1) it clarifies the allegory; (2) it
presents a series of familiar events to the audience so that the

latter can identify itself with the play; (3) it shows that the
Eucharist is the culmination of a long series of events, which
are rather like a crescendo; (4) it permits the author to give the
play the particular direction he desires. For example: in Calderón's *The Supper of King Baltasar*, Baltasar's long speech goes
from verse 222 to verse 579; in his *The Great Theater, The World*,
World's speech covers verses 67-278; and in his *Life is a Dream*
(the sacramental play, not the three-act *comedia* of the same
title) the speech is shared by the Three Divine Persons, Power,
Wisdom, and Love (vv. 258-458). This long speech always comes
at the beginning of the play.

After Echo's long speech, Sor Juana, in order to provide relief
for the audience and prepare it for the main action of the play,
introduces a great deal of spectacle and singing. The stage
directions call for carts to be opened, which reveal Abel lighting
a fire, Enoch at prayer, Abraham sacrificing his son, and Moses
with the Decalogue. These directions follow the example of
Calderón, who used at least five carts in his sacramental plays;
in the more spectacular plays several carts were used simul-
taneously.[5]

Calderón wrote a three-act mythological play called *Echo and
Narcissus*, in which Echo is a shepherdess who loves Narcissus.
In one speech Calderón's Echo tells Narcissus that she is the
richest shepherdess of the valleys and that she will give Narcissus everything if she can be his wife. One stanza of her words,
in Spanish, are these:

> *Eco soy, la más rica*
> *pastora destos valles:*
> *bella decir pudieran*
> *mis infelicidades.*[6]
> (I am Echo, the richest
> shepherdess of these valleys:
> my great unhappiness
> might tell you of my beauty.)

Sor Juana's Echo, in the scene in which she diabolically tempts
Narcissus, tells him that she is the richest shepherdess of the
valleys and that she will give him everything if he will love
(*adorar*) her. One stanza of her words, in Spanish, are these:

> *Eco soy, la más rica*
> *pastora de estos valles:*
> *bella decir pudieran*
> *mis infelicidades.* (vv. 715-718)
> (I am Echo, the richest
> shepherdess of these valleys:
> my great unhappiness
> might tell you of my beauty.)

The reader can see that Sor Juana has used the same stanza, word for word, that Calderón had used before her in his three-act play.

There are other similarities between Sor Juana's sacramental play on Echo and Narcissus and Calderón's mythological play on the same subject: one example is the idea that a beautiful woman, because of her beauty, must be unhappy; another example is the use of the verses known as "echoes" *(ecos)*, which the half-mute Echo recites.[7]

V A *Criticism of* The Divine Narcissus

Although Sor Juana is chiefly known as a lyrical poet and is called at times "The Tenth Muse of Mexico" (an allusion to the original nine muses), the excellence of *The Divine Narcissus* indicates that her greatest talent lay in dramatic rather than lyrical poetry; her theater as a whole, moreover, shows more spontaneity and imagination than most of her poems.

The Divine Narcissus has one or two shortcomings. It seems rather long for a sacramental play, owing to the fact that the first 276 verses are really a *loa* within the play itself; that is, having written a *loa* to *The Divine Narcissus,* Sor Juana follows it up with what is in effect another *loa* in the first 276 verses of the play. The argument between Synagogue and Gentilism has no bearing on the movement of the play but serves only as a prelude to its allegory.

The reader will recall Sor Juana's use of the verses known as "echoes" when the devil Echo has to repeat the last words of those who speak to her; for example, "I Have, Pain, Rage." In spite of their relevancy, the *ecos* run with scarcely any relief from verses 1480 to 1691; they become monotonous and detract from this part of the myth and its translation into Christian theology. One of the principal weaknesses in all of Sor Juana's writings is her indulgence in the fads of her age, such as anagrams, *ecos,* philosophical words, and puns.

VI   *The* Loa *to* The Divine Narcissus

In the Dictionary of the Royal Academy the third meaning of the word *loa* is: a short dramatic composition, with action and plot, which used to be presented before a dramatic poem (play) as a prelude or introduction. The *loa* preceding *The Divine Narcissus* is an example of such a *loa* and it is by far the best that Sor Juana wrote. It is a succinct and spectacular interpretation of the Conquest (the sixteenth century).

VI   *The* Loa *to* The Divine Narcissus

Occident (an Indian youth)	Religion (a Spanish lady)
America (an Indian maid)	Music
Zeal (a Spanish Captain General)	Soldiers
Musicians	

The principal theme of this *loa* is Communion, a comparison of the Aztecs' Communion with the Eucharist Sacrifice of the Christians. The Aztecs took corn flour and mixed it with their blood in order to make an image of their God of Fertility, which they consumed;[8] the Christians, on the other hand, took the body and blood of Christ in the Host, which was a wafer of unleavened bread. These Aztec rites provide the dramatic conflict for Sor Juana's *loa,* in which Occident and America obstinately cling to their religious customs and meet the opposition of Zeal and Religion, who wish to introduce the sacrifice of the Mass. In the *loa* the spectacle of the *tocotín* and the sound of singing and rattles support the young Aztec couple, whereas Spanish soldiers and the sounds of drums and bugles support the two Spaniards.

The *loa* begins with an Indian dance and song, the *tocotín,* in which the men and women wear native garments and carry feathers and rattles to provide the rhythm for the dance. The figure Occident comes forth with America at his side: he is an Indian swain and she a beautiful maid.

The figure called Music speaks to the dancing Indians and urges them on, reminding them that this is a day of commemoration, joy, and festivity on which they are going to pay homage to their god: "and with festive joy/ celebrate the great God of

Fertility." These and similar verses, which recur frequently in the *loa* and also in the last verse (v. 498), emphasize the main theme: the comparison of the Aztecs' Communion with that of the Christians.

The dancing Indians make their exit as Zeal and Religion come to Occident and America to tell them they have a superior doctrine to offer them. Zeal (who is dressed as a Captain General) has already drawn his sword to smite the idolators, but the Spanish lady, Religion, counsels a more moderate course:

> I shall go too, since pity
> persuades me to come
> (ere you attack them with your fury)
> and offer them in peace
> my cult's reception.

The young pagan couple asks Religion who she is. She describes herself and tells them she hopes to convert them to her cult, but they defy both her and Zeal, who as a Captain General has stepped in to help her. Zeal, the secular arm, calls for war:

> Call to arms! War, war! (v. 189)
> (There is the sound of drum and bugles.)
> Long live Spain! Long live her King! (v. 201)

The war scene is brief but spectacular as the Spaniards pursue the Indians on the stage. After the pagans' defeat, Occident says: "Your might must conquer me,/ your reason cannot." Zeal (the General) wishes to punish the obstinacy of Occident (the Indian youth), but Religion steps in and says it is her office to make the pagans surrender through reason, through "persuasive softness."

In the next one hundred and fifty verses (vv. 247-400) the pagans and Religion compare their rites: the Aztecs can eat an image of their god and wash before this meal; the Christians can receive Communion and their washing is called baptism. The pagans are impressed by the Christian rites and wish to know more. Religion realizes that for a simple people a picture is worth a thousand words and so she will teach Occident and America not by abstractions but by a sacramental play:

Let us go.
For in a metaphorical idea
dressed in rhetorical colors
visible to your eye,
I will show you.

Religion will show them *The Divine Narcissus,* which will appeal
to them since it is half Christian and half pagan; it is meeting
them half way.

VII   A *Commentary on This* Loa

First, this *loa* is one of the few instances where Mexico has
furnished the inspiration for Sor Juana's art. The other scenes
from Mexico are in the *villancicos*.

Secondly, although Sor Juana does not mention the *just war*
and the great debates of the sixteenth century concerning the
Conquest, the readers of authors such as Vitoria, Suárez, Las
Casas, and Sepúlveda will realize that these things were in her
mind as she wrote this *loa*. All in all, her attitude towards the
Conquest seems neutral. She shows no recrimination for Zeal,
and yet the pagan Occident and America are not ugly. With
the exception of her praise of the Sacrament, which the audience
must expect in a *loa* for a sacramental play, there is a singular
lack of bias on Sor Juana's part. A critic hestitates to use the
word, since it has nineteenth century connotations, but the *loa*
at times seems realistic; or perhaps ·it is better to say that
Sor Juana assents to both that which is Spanish and that which
is Indian. The Conquest happened, and she accepts it.

Third, the last seventy verses of this *loa* hold some interest for
historians and for Sor Juana's biographers. The Spanish lady,
Religion, tells Zeal that the sacramental play is to be staged in
Madrid rather than Mexico, and that she has written it through
no whim of her own but out of obedience to others. This same
kind of protest, "written at the behest of others," appears in
The Reply to Sor Filotea (see Chapter I.)[9]

VIII   The Martyr of the Sacrament, St. Hermenegildo

The Visigothic kingdom in Spain, which lasted from the beginning of the sixth century until the year 711, held at first
to the Arian religion and its denial of Christ as the eternal Son

of God. There was a severe division between the Arian and Catholic parties in Spain that resulted in civil war, but under King Recaredo (586-601) the kingdom accepted the Catholic religion. This conversion of Recaredo and his followers to Catholicism united the Visigothic rulers and the masses of the people.

Although Recaredo became king, he was not the oldest son of his father, King Leovigildo (568-586). The oldest son had been Hermenegildo who, through the influence of his wife Ingunda and San Leandro, the Bishop of Seville, had converted from Arianism to Catholicism in 579. The Catholic Hermenegildo rebelled against his Arian father; the latter warred against him and exiled him to Valencia.

There is some discrepancy in historical documents concerning the death of Hermenegildo. Not all the chroniclers picture him as a martyr, but Gregory the Great says that he was put to death at the order of his father, Leovigildo, for refusing to receive Communion from the hands of an Arian bishop. This version of Hermenegildo's death, with its emphasis on the sacrament of the Eucharist, is the pith of Sor Juana's sacramental play, *The Marytr, St. Hermenegildo.*[10]

The Cast of Characters

San Hermenegildo	Mercy
Leovigildo, his father	Justice
Recaredo, his brother	Truth
Geserico, an ambassador	Peace
Ingunda, the saint's wife	Spain
Apostasy	Fame
Musicians	Soldiers
San Leandro	Fantasy
Faith	Many people

The Gothic Kings

The major action of the play is the struggle between the Arian and Catholic parties in Visigothic Spain as personified in the fight and martyrdom of Hermenegildo.

Hermenegildo is faced with the problem that troubles all leaders at one time or another: what is a man to do when both sides of a dispute he must settle have a just argument? Her-

menegildo loves his father, Leovigildo, and since both Natural
and Revealed Law (vv. 190-93) order a man to honor his
parents, is it right for him to wage war on his father? On the
other hand, Christ has said a man must leave all for Him—father,
mother, life itself (vv. 106-9; 827-30)—when His love demands it.
Is is right for Hermenegildo to submit to Leovigildo, who is
using his power to advance the false Arian religion in Spain?
This conflict runs all through the play and constitutes its unity.
The audience witnesses the solution of the conflict at the end
of the play, when Hermenegildo chooses martyrdom rather than
receive the Sacrament from the hands of an Arian bishop. The
bishop is acting at the orders of Leovigildo whose son, by refusing
to receive Communion from him, is giving up his father and
his life for Christ.

IX A Criticism of the Play

In order to criticize The Martyr, St. Hermenegildo it is necessary to discuss at some length the nature of the auto sacramental,
the one-act sacramental play, and the comedia, the three-act play.

In his introduction to Calderón's sacramental plays, Angel
Valbuena Prat shows the essential difference between the Spanish
comedia and the Spanish auto sacramental. The basic structure
of the comedia was fixed by Lope de Vega:

Lope de Vega set the model for the Spanish comedia. A broad picture
of human life such as it appeared in the national society of his age, it
included what was heroic, courtly and popular. The three acts that
he divided his comedias into and his technique of a variety of scenes
are well suited to a complicated action filled with diverse elements,
with different characters that are usually sketched rather than an-
alyzed, and with lively, rapid passions such as those of the author
himself; and . . . in most cases intrigues are mixed in also. There are
frequently many characters in his plays, and it is hard for one of them
to corner our attention.

In Calderón there is a tendency to confine the characters and
the action, a tendency toward a one-act play, even though he
continues the tradition of the three-act comedia established by
Lope de Vega. Calderón becomes the master of the auto
sacramental:

Two different styles stand out in the theater of Calderón: one that continues and perfects the realistic sense of the drama of Lope and his contemporaries . . . The second style in Calderón, which is more original and in many respects closer to us, is to be found in his religio-philosophical plays *(comedias)*, his mythological plays *(comedias)*, and his sacramental plays *(autos)*. Here is a new genre in which the ideas, the poetry of the subject matter and the poetic form itself, and the use at times of music, take precedence over the elements of his first style. Hence we can say that Calderón created the sacramental play *(auto)*, just as Lope lay down the structure of the Spanish play *(comedia)*. For Calderón one act is sufficient, one act sufficiently long for him to develop his transcendent theme; that is why he will broaden it as much as he has to, but he will not start a second act. . . . He can develop the main interest within the confines of one longer act.[11]

If the reader applies these ideas of Valbuena Prat to Sor Juana's *The Martyr of the Sacrament, St. Hermenegildo,* he will see that her play lacks the comparatively intense unity of a sacramental play. There is a dichotomy in *St. Hermenegildo* that detracts from its hold on the audience.

On the one hand, parts of the play resemble one of the less impressive *loas* of Sor Juana. The abstract *figures*—Faith, Mercy, Justice, Truth, Peace, the Virtues—appear in scenes that are in effect a prologue (vv. 1-213) and an epilogue (vv. 1907-62). Their other appearance in the play either disrupt the action or are such that they could be assumed by a character from a play *(comedia)* about a saint's life. For example, when Hermenegildo must decide whether or not to war with his father (vv. 214-344), two of the Virtues urge peace and two urge war; since they merely repeat the arguments of Hermenegildo himself and do not intensify the struggle going on in his breast, they might better have been substituted by a lesser number of characters. Later on the Virtues disrupt the action of the play (vv. 1259-1374); their lines continue the altercation they began back in vv. 1-213, and their struggle adds nothing to the major action of the play, which is the struggle between the Arian and Catholic parties in Spain as personified in Hermenegildo.

The other half of the dichotomy, which takes up about 1600 verses, tells the story of Hermenegildo and the Arian party in Spain. This story does not have the characteristics of a sacramental play. Leovigildo's ambassador Geserico has a long speech at the beginning (vv. 363-602), but it is not allegorical and has nothing to do with scenes from the Old Testament. Geserico traces the history of the Visigoths from long before Alarico to Leovigildo, the sixteenth king, and argues that the Arian religion has always been a mainstay of the Visigothic state; consequently, he says, Hermenegildo should not change his religion.

Furthermore, none of the other characters in this play strikes the reader as allegorical. Recaredo urges his brother Hermenegildo to give in to their father and counsels moderation on the grounds that he can peacefully change the Visigoths' religion when he becomes king. Hermenegildo's wife Ingunda is sent as a hostage to the emperor Tiberius (who does not appear in the play) in exchange for the latter's aid; her purpose in the play is to emphasize the noble character of Hermenegildo and to add to the theme that a follower of Christ will give up father, spouse, and life itself if it is God's will.

The abstract Fantasy is not allegorical but only a figure Sor Juana uses to goad Leovigildo against his son. Fantasy briefly exhorts Leovigildo to take vengeance in order to vindicate Arianism, from which the king derives his glory. Right after Fantasy's speech, another figure, Fame, comes and passes all the Visigothic kings in review before the eyes of Leovigildo (vv. 933-1048). This spectacle, whose purpose is to stir up Visigothic-Arian feelings in Leovigildo's breast, is not a religious pageant like the scene in *The Divine Narcissus* (vv. 539-94) in which Abel, Enoch, Abraham, and Moses passed before the audience.

Even the figure called Apostasy is not allegorical: he is the prelate of the Arians and memorable as the persecutor of Hermenegildo. In other words, the play is concrete rather than figurative, historical rather than metaphorical.

In conclusion, Sor Juana's *The Martyr, St. Hermenegildo* is not so much a sacramental play as an inchoate three-act play about the life of a saint.[12]

X   El cetro de José (Joseph's Scepter)

The play begins with a short scene in which the brothers of Joseph decide first to kill him and then to sell him into slavery. After they leave, the devil, Lucero, appears with his perpetual companions, Intelligence, Knowledge, Envy, and Conjecture.

From their words the audience learns that the story of Joseph is the foretoken of a great mystery and that he is the precursor of someone. The devil with his great Intelligence will strive to grasp the meaning of this mystery, but in vain.

The devil and his friends are joined by the voice of Music, the "voice of God," which comes from offstage and sings of three spectacular events. The stage directions read:

(The cart that represents Paradise is opened, and there are Adam and Eve . . .)
(The cart with Adam and Eve is closed; and that of Abraham is opened; it has a heaven of stars . . .)
(Another cart is opened; and inside is Jacob, asleep at the foot of the Ladder, and above there is The Lord . . .)

The story of Joseph himself begins with his temptation by the wife of Putiphar (vv. 354-78). She speaks of her great beauty, and should it fail to move Joseph:

> let a soul in surrender move you;
> for the treasures of the soul
> do not pay wages to time,
> nor tribute to changes!
> Don't flee, Joseph, wait:
> turn at least your face;
> look at me, for with your glance
> you do not stain your fidelity.
> Turn your eyes!

The wife appeals to Joseph's pride ("let a soul in surrender move you"), which is the most telling of temptations. She also attacks Joseph through his body, because she knows that if her beauty can capture his eyes, she can capture his soul. Joseph, however, refuses her and, consoled by the figure Prophecy, he flees this proximate occasion of sin. Putiphar's wife is in league with Lucero, the devil, and at his advice bears false witness against Joseph, which accounts for his being in jail later on when the Pharaoh anxiously seeks an interpretation of his dreams.

Joseph is able to foretell the future, which is a miracle above nature, because his mind is illuminated by God's grace:

PROPHECY
Let your enlightened mind
soar beyond itself,
since you have as a boon
divine assistance. (vv. 690-93)

Joseph's aplomb and his miraculous prediction of the seven fat
years and the seven lean years contrasts dramatically with the
consternation of Lucero who, although his Intelligence is vastly
superior to Joseph's cannot unfathom the dream. The despair of
the devil emphasizes the hope of man and his ability to look for
good tidings in the future. Redemption! The sacramental plays
extol the virtue of Hope more than any other.

After Joseph's interpretation of the Pharaoh's dream, the allusions to man's redemption and the Sacrament keep growing. The
people of Egypt (who are represented by Music) call Joseph
"the Saviour of the World"; Lucero, the devil, knows that "God
wills to redeem the world"; because there is famine in Canaan;
Jacob sends his sons to Egypt, for "they sell Wheat in Egypt";
Prophecy speaks of a "Sovereign Wheat" (these references to
Wheat are allusions to the Holy Eucharist, which is made of
wheat); the people of Egypt shout out to Joseph:

You are the Father of our country,
and as such, our Father,
Give us our daily Bread. (vv. 929-31)

These words clearly refer to the Lord's Prayer.

Prophecy, moreover, shows that Joseph is not only a historical
person but also a symbolical one, and God had several reasons
for desiring that his story be known to men: Joseph serves as a
comparison to Christ; the story of Joseph holds hope for mankind; and the history of Joseph acts as a kind of proof for the
mysteries of the New Testament, since it foretells them. In a
word, the reason for Joseph's experiences is

that the World might see in him
of the Saviour the living Idea. (vv. 911-12)

The remaining seven-hundred-odd verses of this sacramental
play continue the three major themes that have already been
established: Joseph—Christ; Bread, Wheat, Tassels, the dinner

of Joseph and his twelve brothers—the Holy Eucharist, the Last
Supper of Christ and his twelve apostles; the devil's conflict and
despair—man's redemption. At the end, the stage directions call
for the customary spectacle of a chalice and a host, and Prophecy
alone remains on the stage. She sums up the meaning of the play.
The Old Law has become the New:

> *y ya, transcendiendo siglos,*
> *la que allá fuí Profecía,*
> *a ser aquí Fe he venido,*
> *sin que cause disonancia:*
> *pues un acto es de Fe mismo*
> *dar crédito a lo futuro*
> *que dársela a lo no visto;*
> *pues lo mismo es creer en Dios*
> *que creer porque Dios lo dijo*
> *creyendo allá contra el tiempo,*
> *y aquí contra los sentidos* . . . (vv. 1611-21)
> (and now, with centuries gone by,
> I who was Prophecy there,
> have here become Faith,
> with no ground for dissonance:
> since it is the same act of Faith
> to give credence to what is future
> as to give it to the unseen;
> since it is the same to believe in God
> as to believe because God has said it,
> for then they believed against time,
> as now they believe against the senses.)

At the very end Prophecy praises the Sacrament amidst two
Choruses of Music.

XI *Conclusion*

In her religious theater, Sor Juana has captured the redemptive
spirit of the sacramental plays in *The Divine Narcissus* and
Joseph's Scepter. The reader witnesses the drama of a human
being caught between evil and vices on the one hand and Christ's
promise of salvation on the other. These dramas extol the theological virtue of Hope. *The Martyr, St. Hermenegildo,* however,
is rather ill defined and resembles a three-act play *(comedia)*
of a saint's life more than it does a sacramental play.

CHAPTER 5

The Poetry of Sor Juana

I *The* Villancicos

S OR Juana was in effect a poet laureate who had to write many poems for the important occasions of Church and State. For the Church she wrote a series of *villancicos* celebrating certain feast days of the year. Most of them were to be combined with the prayers of matins, and a few were to be sung at the Epistle, the Offertory, and the *Ite missa est* of the Mass.

Those *villancicos* that were written as "complete sets for matins" were broken up into three nocturnes matching the three parts of matins. The first nocturne had the task of introducing the mystery of the feast day or the history of the saint whose memory was being celebrated. The second nocturne was generally less grave and drew images from the arts and sciences: medicine, music, fencing, astronomy, philosophy, teaching, painting, physics, and history. In most cases the second nocturne also had the *jácara*, a lively piece that provided relief for the congregation. In the *villancicos* for the Immaculate Conception, 1689, Sor Juana describes the purpose of the *jácara*; the chorus has sung very well and now: "one singer alone wanted/ in a jacarandina/ to soothe with levity/ the gravity of the tones."

The third nocturne had the remaining two poems of the set and usually repeated a previous theme. One of these poems was the *ensalada*, a mixture of verses that were for the most part frivolous. Nevertheless, it is the *ensalada* that has the one durable part of all these *villancicos*,[1] the poetry of the Negro.

The Negroes appear in the following verses of the *villancicos*: Assumption 1676, VIII; Immaculate Conception 1676, VIII; St. Peter Nolasco 1677, VIII; Assumption 1679, VIII; Assumption 1685, VIII; St. Joseph 1690, VIII. The purpose of the Negro verses was to amuse a congregation that was tired after a long time at prayer, but in effect they capture the religious spirit of the occasion better than the other verses.

The Church preaches the gospel of the uncircumcision, which is not confined to any nation because of its purity of blood,[2] superior law, politics, economics, or philosophy. The gospel is meant for all, the meanest slave and the greatest king. And so the Negroes can sing to their mother Mary, who is also the mother of God.

The Feast of the Assumption 1676

The Spanish of the Negroes	The same verses in ordinary Spanish.	An English translation.
1. *Cantemo, Pilico, que se va las Reina*	1. *Cantemos, Perico, que se va la Reina*	1. Petey, let's sing, the Queen is going away
y dalemu turo una noche buena.	*y démosle todos una noche buena.*	let us all bid her good night.
2. *Iguale yolale Flacico, de pena, que nos deja ascula*	2. *Igual es llorar Blasico, de pena, que nos deja oscuros*	2. Better to cry Blaisey, from sorrow since she leaves us dark (in darkness)
a turo las negla.	*a todos los negros.*	all us Negroes.
1. *Si las Cielo va*	1. *Si al Cielo va*	1. If she's going to Heaven
y Dioso la lleva	*y Dios se la lleva*	and God takes her away
¿pala qué yolá si Eya sa cuntenta?	*¿para qué llorar si Ella está contenta?*	why should we cry if She is happy?
Sará muy galana vitita ri tela milando la Sole pisando la Streya.	*Estará muy galana vestida de tela mirando el Sol pisando las Estrellas.*	She must be beautiful dressed up in silk seeing the Sun walking the Stars.
2. *Déjame yolá Flacico por Eya que se va, y nosotlo la Oblaje nos deja.*	2. *Déjame llorar Blasico por Ella que se va y nosotros el Obraje nos deja.*	2. Let me cry Blaisey for her for she's going and she leaves us the workhouse.
1. *Caya, que sa siempre*	1. *Calla, que está siempre*	1. Quiet, she will always

milando la Iglesia;	*mirando la Iglesia;*	be watching the Church;
mila las Pañola	*mira a la Española*	look at the Spanish lady
que se quela plieta.	*que se queda prieta* (or *apretada*).	how somber she is.
2. *Bien dici, Flacico*	2. *Bien dices, Blasico*	2. You are right, Blaisey
tura sa suspensa;	*toda está suspensa;*	she is all amazed;
si tú quiele, demo	*si tú quieres, demos*	if you want, let us
unas cantaleta.	*una cantaleta.*	sing in jest.
1. *Nomble de mi Dioso*	1. *Nombre de mi Dios*	1. By God's name
que sa cosa buena!	*que es cosa buena!*	that's a good idea!
Aola, Pilico	*Ahora, Perico*	Now, Petey
que nos mila atenta.	*que nos mira atenta.*	since she's looking at us.
Estribillo	*Estribillo*	Refrain
¡Ah, ah, ah,	*¡Ah, ah, ah,*	Ah, ah, ah,
que la Reina se nos va!	*que la Reina se nos va!*	the Queen has gone and left us!
¡Uh, uh, uh,	*¡Uh, uh, uh,*	Hu, hu, hu,
que non blanca como tú,	*que no es blanca como tú*	She is not white like you,
nin Pañó que no sa buena,	*ni Española que no es buena*	nor Spanish, which is not good,
que Eya dici: So molena	*que Ella dice: soy morena*	cause she says I am d∼k
con las Sole que mirá!	*con el Sol que me miró!*	from the Sun that looked on me!
¡Ah, ah, ah,	*¡Ah, ah, ah,*	Ah, ah, ah,
que la Reina se nos va!	*que la Reina se nos va!*	the Queen has gone and left us!

Here is the sentiment of the poor and downtrodden. The Queen has gone to heaven where she's looking after all her friends, not just the people from high society. She is a dark queen (la Virgen Morena) who has a special love for Petey and Blaisey. Even for the poor, life is a comedy.

In the last *villancico* of the Immaculate Conception 1676 series, a Negro sings his praises of the Virgin. He is happy and he is singing because he knows how to praise his queen as well as the next man:

Acá tamo tolo	All we mixed bloods *(zambos)*
Zambio, lela, lela,	Are here, lela, lela,
que tambié sabemos	cause we too know how
cantaye las Leina.	to sing to the Queen.

He is told to go away on this feast of purity and light, for anything black doesn't fit in with the celebration. But he answers:

Aunque neglo, blanco	Although black, we are
somo, lela, lela,	white, lela, lela,
que el alma rivota	cause the good soul
blanca sa, no prieta.	is white, not black.

There is no stopping this fellow. The rest of the verses are his. The devil grew bold and tried to harm the Virgin, but she gave that scoundrel (dirty dog) just what he deserved.

The *villancicos* of St. Peter Nolasco 1677 also show the feeling of the Negroes towards the whites. The black man is the poor man who works hard for little pay. He has heard that St. Peter Nolasco redeems the slaves but he cannot believe he did anything for the blacks because he knows from experience the whites get all the good things and live up there in that palace. In a primitive way his thought is very cynical and uncharitable, and the Negro repents for having had it:

La otra noche con mi conga	The other night with my wife
turo sin durmi pensaba	I couldn't sleep and thought
que no quiele gente plieta	he doesn't like black people
como eya so gente branca.	as well as his own white.
Sola saca la Pañola;	He only helps the Spaniard;
¡pues, Dioso, mila la trampa	well, God, see the hitch
que aunque neglo gente somo	cause we are people,
	though we're black
aunque nos dici cabaya!	though they call us *burro!*
Mas ¿qué digo, Dioso mío?	But what am I saying, God?
¡Los demoño, que me engaña,	the devil he deceives me,
pala que esé mulmulando	to make me gossip
a esa Redentola Santa!	about that redeeming Saint.

El Santo me lo perrone,   I hope the Saint will pardon me,
que só una malo hablala,   and all my evil chatter
que aunque padesca la cuepo   for though the body suffers
en ese libla las almá.   that's what frees the soul.

In the Assumption 1679 series of *villancicos* there are two
princesses from Guinea with bundles, who are on their way to
market. These salesládies put down their bundles and start to
sing:

2. *Dejemoso la cocina*   Let us leave the food
y vamoso a turo trote,   and go as fast as we can
sin que vindamos gamote   without selling sweets (potatoes)
nin garbanzo a la vizina: or chickpeas to the women:
qui arto gamote, Cristina,   for many sweets, Christina,
hoy a la fieta vendrá.   will come to the fiesta today.

The Lady Mary ("Ledy Melly") was a good slave and that's why
they freed her and sent her up to heaven:

Milala como cohete   See her like a skyrocket
que va subiendo lo sumo.   climbing in the sky.

For the theologian the Assumption is a mystery of Faith that
demands careful study, but for these two princesses with their
graphic minds the Assumption is like the path of a skyrocket.
   In the Assumption 1685 series the *camotero* (vendor of sweet
potatoes) is a man on very personal terms with his heavenly
mother. He would never think of calling himself "one of the
faithful," but only "your black Tony" (tu negro Antón), and
he asks Mary to wait before ascending until he can bring his
gifts to her:

Espela, aun no suba,   Wait, don't go yet
que to negro Antón   for your black Tony
te guarra cuajala   has curds for you
branca como Sol.   white as the Sun.

God must delay His plan in History until Antón can deliver his
salted chickpeas, fine sweets, and curds to his mother, Mary.
Like the two princesses of Guinea, Antón has a graphic way of
saying things. Who but he would think to say:

¡Oh Santa María	Oh Holy Mary,
que a Dioso parió	who delivered God
sin haber comadre	without a midwife
ni tené doló!	or labor pains!

The Negro verses appear in the last *villancico* of each set. Of all the verses they alone have preserved for us the religious meaning of the occasion.

II A Criticism of the Villancicos[3]

A good many poems that Sor Juana composed for State occasions (the birthday of the king, the birthday of the viceroy, and so forth) will not stand the test of literary criticism; the same may be said of the *villancicos,* which she wrote for Church occasions. Sor Juana led a liturgical life, of which the feasts of the *villancicos* were a part, and so they have a certain sincerity and genuineness not to be found in many of her secular pieces; nevertheless, they are not poetry.

The *villancicos* rely too much on paradoxes and other trick devices. If the reader will picture for a moment the Cathedral of Mexico or Puebla in the early hours of the morning with the choir and religious singing the prayers of matins, he can see the problem of the nun. In between antiphon, psalm, and lesson, she had to supply *villancicos* that were also to be sung, and she could not appeal to the eyes of those present but only to their ears, since the *villancicos* do not provide the spectacle of theater. Sor Juana had to create means of attracting and holding attention.

Thus she puts a paradox in one of her poems: did the Blessed Mother descend or ascend when she was assumed into heaven? She ascended with joy into the arms of her Son; "the rest was a descent." (Feast of the Assumption 1690, *Villancico* I, v. 70)

Another paradox is the bet between St. Joseph and God, and the idea that Joseph wakes up when he sleeps, because an angel reveals to him in a dream that his virgin wife is to bear the Son of God. (Feast of St. Joseph 1690, *Villancicos* VI and XI.

Another trick device is an enigma or riddle:

—I shall propose a riddle.
—And I shall answer it.

One singer argues that the Feast of the Assumption is August 15, and another argues that it is March 25 (the Incarnation) because the real assumption or rising of the Mother of God was her union with Christ. Perhaps no theologian will object to this argument but the literary critic will have to agree with Menéndez Pelayo, who called these verses mental gymnastics and disapproved of them.

In some of the *villancicos* Sor Juana mixed Spanish and Nahuatl, or Spanish and Latin:

> *Yo al Santo lo tengo*
> *mucha devoción,*
> *y de Sempual Xuchil*
> *un Xuchil le doy.*
> (Feast of St. Peter Nolasco 1677, *Villancico* VIII)
> *Tristes te invocamus:*
> *concede, gloriosa,*
> *gratias quae te illustrant,*
> *dotes quae te adornant.*
> (Feast of the Assumption 1679, *Villancico II*)

The *villancicos* are important documents for the biographer of Sor Juana and for the historian of the seventeenth century. One of the *villancicos* is written with the simplicity of a catechism (Feast of the Immaculate Conception 1676, *Villancico* III); another shows that Sor Juana knew the doctrines of latria and hyperdulia (Conception 1676, *Villancico* VI); another shows she knew the procedure of a Scholastic debate (St. Peter the Apostle 1677, *Villancico* VI); in another she applies the idea of hylomorphism to the Assumption. There are scores of ideas and expressions such as those just mentioned in the two-hundred-odd pages of the *villancicos*. As for the historian, he will find many social and cultural references in these verses: a Negro vendor of sweet potatoes; a Biscayan; two sacristans; an idea from physics; an image from the science of the day; the translation of the Bible by the Seventy-Two, comparisons from music, rhetoric, teaching, philosophy, and fencing; some Portuguese; even a reference to the *mal francés!*

III *The Lyrical Poetry*

The lyrical poetry of Sor Juana consists of metrical combinations known as *romances, endechas, redondillas, décimas, glosas, sonetos, liras, ovillejos,* and *silvas.* A careful reading of this lyrical poetry will show that it can be divided into three parts: (A) the courtly poems, that is, poems Sor Juana wrote for the viceroy's court, for dignitaries, or for the king; (B) the love poems; and (C) thirteen sonnets.

A. *The Courtly Poems*

The courtly poems, which comprise about three-fourths of Sor Juana's lyrical poetry, are not distinguished verses. Some of these poems are for an archbishop, a marchesa, the viceroy, the king, a young doctor; others are based on an anagram; others are written in Latin or translate a Latin poem; others praise contemporaries of Sor Juana and ask them for verses. Other courtly poems accompany a gift Sor Juana is sending to a friend; they answer the poem of another writer; they are entries in a poetic contest; or they play with the language of Scholastic philosophy. Most of these poems are little more than clever exercises.

Occasionally the reader comes upon some good verses in the courtly poems; for example, the following lines from the *romance* "Si daros los buenos años," which was presented to the viceroy on his birthday:

> Grey hairs must be sought
> before they are painted by time:
> whoever would have them finds joy,
> affliction whoever awaits them.
> The fool who finally walks
> the premise of old age,
> combs shame rather than locks,
> repeats outrages rather than years.
> The wise young man in short
> leaves an eternal frame
> for his Life, and with his fame
> marks eternity. (See Alfonso Méndez Plancarte,
> *Obras completas de Sor Juana,* vol. I, p. 47.
> Henceforth I shall refer to this work by writing
> *MP,* the volume, and the page.)

B. *The Love Poems*

The second group consists of some fifty love poems, about a fifth of Sor Juana's lyrical poetry. Most of these are as undistinguished as the courtly poems, but a dozen of them are worthwhile and two are excellent. The better love poems seem to come from Sor Juana's own experience rather than from an occasion of Church or State, or from a literary fashion of the day, such as an anagram or a polite poetical debate.

The *romances* are the least inspired of Sor Juana's love poems and do not impart any personal warmth. They deal with themes that border on the philosophical; for example, the poem "Supuesto, discurso mío" argues the problem of love and disdain. The poetess loves Fabio, who does not return her love, and she is loved by Silvio, for whom she has no feeling. What is she to do? Is she obligated to Silvio?

> Is it not harsh, not tyranny
> the passions being the same,
> his lack of self-restraint
> and his desire that I myself restrain?
>
> To love him because he loves me
> is not rightly called love,
> for he loves not, who supposes
> that to love he must be loved.
> Love is not correspondence;
> .   .   .   .
> And indeed, though so much truth
> were wanting on my behalf,
> my will belongs to Fabio,
> Silvio and the world please pardon. (MP, I, 20)

In the *romance* "Ya que para despedirme" the theme is the absence of the lover. This absence and the jealousy accompanying it are the most common themes in the *romances*, and they carry over into the sonnets and *endechas*. For example, in the *endecha* "Prolija memoria," the reader comes upon the lines:

> Why do you air
> the idle question,
> whether inconstancy
> be the child of absence?
> I well know the frailty
> of nature
> whose one constancy
> is to be not so. (MP, I, 190)

The *endechas* are rather better than the *romances*, but they do not measure up to Sor Juana's sonnets and *liras*. For example, in the poem "Si acaso, Fabio mío" the reader finds these lines:

> hear, in this sad dirge
> the tender harmony
> that soothes, a funeral rite,
> the dying swan.
> And ere eternal Night
> with deadly opaque key
> the dim light snuffs
> of my fainthearted eyes,
> give me the last embrace,
> whose tender ties
> unify bodies,
> thus identify souls.
> Let night hear thy sweet voice
> and let it not smother
> in troubled cadence,
> thy words entire.
> From thy countenance on mine
> make in love an image
> and bathe these frigid cheeks
> with ardent tears. (MP, I, 201)

Although these verses show more warmth than the *romances*, they retain a certain intellectual aloofness. In the lines "unify bodies/ thus identify souls" ("siendo unión de los cuerpos/ identifican almas") the thought would have made a splendid verse if it had not been expressed so prosaically. Once again Sor Juana is abusing the language of philosophy.

The two best sonnets are "Esta tarde, mi bien, cuando te hablaba," and the "Detente, sombra de mi bien esquivo":

> This eve, my love, when I spoke with thee
> I saw by thy gesture and face
> How with words I could not move thee
> And I wanted thee to see my heart.
> And Love, who helped my design
> Conquered what seemed scant of gain
> For amongst the tears that sorrow poured
> My heart fell in drops undone.
> No more rigor, my love, no more;

Jealous tyrants need torment thee no more,
Nor vile suspicion test thy quietude
With foolish shades, with empty clue,
Since in liquid humor thou hast seen and touched
My heart between thy hands undone. (MP, I, 287)

Hold on, shade of my evasive love,
Image of the spell I most adore,
Fair illusion for which happily I die,
Sweet fiction for which painfully I live.
If for the lodestone of thy grace
My breast serves, obedient steel,
Why must thou please and enamor,
If fleeting thou willst to fool me?
But thou may not boast self-satisfied
That thy tyranny vanquished me,
For though thou leavest the close tie deceived,
Which thy fantastic form has wound,
It little matters thou foolest arms and breast
If my phantasy has captured thee in chains. (MP, I, 287)

In many of the other sonnets Sor Juana unfortunately returns to the clever manner of the *romances*, for example:

He who ungrateful leaves me, lovingly I seek;
He who lovingly seeks me, ungratefully I leave;
Constant I adore him who disdains my love;
I disdain him who constantly seeks my love. (MP, I, 289)

For the present writer, the best of Sor Juana's love poems is the one called "Amado dueño mío," which is written in *liras*. This poem expresses the feelings that come from the absence of the loved one. Here are some selections:

My beloved lord,
Hear a while my tired lament
which I to the wind confide
that quickly it might reach thine ear
if the dolorous plaint does not vanish
like my hope, in air. (vv. 1-6)
If thou seest the loquacious stream
woo the meadow's flowers,
a pleasing lover that charms

and tells them of his care,
my grief will have thee know
how his current laughs fed by mine own woe. (vv. 19-24)
If thou seest the wounded stag
down the mountain, hurried,
seeking anguished
ease in a frozen stream,
and thirsty plunge the waters,
in anguish not ease he follows me. (vv. 37-42)
If thou seest clear the sky
such is the candor of my soul;
and if, avaricious of light
the day is veiled with gloom,
it is in inclement obscurity
the image of thine absence and my life. (vv. 49-54)
When will thy sonorous voice
wound these ears;
and when will the soul that loves thee,
drowned in joy's delights,
abandon these eyes to laughter
as it hastens from them to greet thee. (vv. 67-72)
When shall I behold the gracious line
of thy quiet countenance
and that unspoken joy,
beyond the pale of human pen,
for all is ill defined
that does not fit experience. (vv. 79-85), (MP, I, 313)

C. *The Philosophical and Historical Sonnets*

The rest of Sor Juana's lyrical poetry consists of thirteen sonnets with philosophical or historical themes. The eight philosophical sonnets repeat the theme of man's return to dust; one of them combines the *return to dust* with the theme of *carpe diem (seize the day)*. Here are three of these sonnets:
[This sonnet concerns a portrait of Sor Juana]

This hued deceit thou seest,
which boasting art's comeliness
with colors' false syllogism
is a delusive betrayal of sense;
yes this, where flattery has thought
to reprieve the horrors of years,
and by subduing time's arrogance

to triumph over age and oblivion,
is esteem's vain dissimulation
is a fragile flower to the wind
is a useless refuge against fate
is foolish errant diligence
is decrepit care, and understood,
is corpse, is dust, is shade, is nought. (MP, I, 277)

[This sonnet is a stricture for a rose, and for those like a rose.]

Rose divine in tender bloom,
thou art in thy fragrant grace
beauty's teacher, born to the purple,
a white snow tenet of comeliness.
Model of the human form
example of charm's emptiness
in whose being nature has joined
the happy cradle and wan sepulchre.
How haughty is thy pomp, how presumptuous,
how proud, thou scornest the threat of death
and later, faint and withdrawn,
of thy withered self givest the despondent sign,
for in foolish life and wise demise
thou teachest dying and living showest deceit. (MP, I, 278)

[This sonnet says that Death is better than exposure to the outrages of old age.]

Celia watched a meadow rose
happily boasting empty splendor,
while with carmine salve and scarlet
it bathed its soft made countenance;
and she said—Enjoy with no fear of Fate
thy buoyant years' quick course
for tomorrow's death cannot quit
what today thou hast possessed;
and though death will come now soon
and thy scented life will away,
thou shalt not mind thy dying, so beautiful, so gay:
see how experience teaches thee
thou art fortunate dying in bloom
not knowing old age's vehemence. (MP, I, 278)

There are five historic-mythological sonnets, which concern women from antiquity. Two of them praise the gallant Lucretia, a favorite of Sor Juana, who fought so bravely to preserve her purity against the lecherous Tarquino. The best of these sonnets is about Pyramus and Thisbe.

Pyramus and Thisbe appear in the *Metamorphoses* of Ovid. They were legendary lovers of Babylon who spoke to each other through an opening in a wall between their houses. One night they planned to meet by a white mulberry tree. Thisbe arrived first at the tree but fled when she saw a lioness. She left a blood-smeared garment, which Pyramus found. Thinking her dead, he took his own life with a sword, and she, on returning, did the same by plunging the weapon into her breast. Pyramus' blood caused the white mulberries to turn red, and Thisbe's, mixed with his, caused them to turn purple.

Here is Sor Juana's sonnet on their tragic love:

> Of a mournful mulberry the black shade,
> of a thousand horrors and confusions full,
> in whose hollow trunk today there still resounds
> the echo that sorrowfully invokes the name of Thisbe;
> this shade covered the green-hued carpet
> where Pyramus in love opened the vein
> of his heart, and This be in her pain
> made the mark that still astounds the world.
> But seeing Love in so great affliction,
> Death took pity on them
> and joined their breast in one tight bond.
> Alas, poor and unhappy is she
> who offers not her breast to her own Pyramus
> not even for a sword's hard blade. (MP, I, 283)

IV Nature in the Poetry of Sor Juana

A writer's attitude towards nature is important since it throws light on the ultimate meaning of his literature. The writings of Sor Juana Inés reveal that her basic attitude towards nature comes from Scholasticism, the doctrine of the medieval school and Golden Age Spain. Sor Juana may have exalted nature in *The Dream* and in some of her other verses, for example the passage in which Echo tempts Narcissus with her possessions, but it is Scholasticism that permeates everything she wrote.

Nature in Scholastic philosophy has a strict order of inanimate matter, vegetable life, sensitive life, and rational life. These various levels of being come under the Aristotelian doctrine of hylomorphism, according to which all bodies consist of two essential principles, matter and form. In her *loa* to Friar Diego Velázquez, Sor Juana has a figure called Nature say: "since I am Nature/ in common, to whose wise/ always operative idea/ the sweet union/ of matter and form is due. . . . In short I am she/ who makes the vegetal grow/ the rational discourse/ the sensitive to feel" (MP, III, 484).

The language of hylomorphism appears in *The Divine Narcissus*. Here is an example: In the era before Christ's coming, Gentilism (the pagan world) has an argument with Synagogue (the world that knows divine revelation). Gentilism has many beautiful myths and stories to tell, but Synagogue has the truth. It would be nice if they could come to some sort of an agreement. Gentilism says that she will provide the *matter* for a sacramental play if Synagogue will supply the *form* or meaning. She concludes her speech to Synagogue: "I do not understand you well, but since you propose that I give you the matter so that you may inform it with another soul, another meaning my eyes do not recognize, I shall give you from my literature the poetic beauty of the story of Narcissus" (MP, III, 27). ("So that you may inform it with another soul": according to hylomorphism, the form of a living being is its soul.)

According to Scholasticism there is a strict order within every part of nature. All material beings are composed of matter and form, that is, informed matter. Forms, however, differ in dignity and the resultant beings fall into a hierarchy:[4]

> Man   — rational form (spiritual soul)
> Animals   — sensitive form (material soul)
> Plants   — vegetable form (material soul)
> Minerals — a non-vital form.

The reader has seen that Sor Juana brings up this doctrine in *The Dream* (Chapter 2). Furthermore, Sor Juana frequently uses the word "order" to describe nature. In the third *loa* for the birthday of the king she writes: "For he [the king] who from the common order/ is exempt,/ does not need years/ to be wise" (MP, III, 325). Sor Juana is saying here that owing to the order of nature all men must have sense perception and experience if they are to acquire knowledge; that is, they must grow old in years to become wise. The glorious king, however, does not need to grow in years to acquire knowledge and wisdom since he is above nature. Sor Juana is exercising a poetic license in order to praise the king. She does not mean to be taken literally.

Sor Juana's attitude towards nature has an effect on her attitude towards the social order. Society has a strict hierarchy. This explains Sor Juana's, profound respect for the monarchy in all the *loas*.

Scholastic theology also sees an order in nature, but it allows for God's taking exception to that order. In the first *loa*, to Charles II, the figure called Love says that the various figures in the poem must speak according to their grade and must keep "the natural order the powerful Hand of God put on us when He took us out of Chaos" (MP, III, 284). Love is talking here about Fire, Air, Water, and Earth, the four elements who must praise King Charles in their natural order. This order in nature is extremely important to Sor Juana.

Nature is the creation of God and its main purpose is to reflect the Beauty of the Creator,[5] to follow Him. He is nature's polestar:

If you can in Narcissus [he has not yet become Christ in the play]
so much perfection suppose,
for you say his beauty is
of hearts the lodestone
and that nymphs and shepherds follow him
and not these alone
but birds and beasts
mountains, dales
streams and fountains
meadows, trees and flowers;
with how much greater truth
is this high perfection
seen in God
for whose Beauty the Spheres
in mirrors' guise
behold themselves unworthy;
and for Whom all creatures
(though there were not cause

of so many gifts
and marvellous favors)
for His Beauty alone
would owe Him adoration
and Whom Nature
(that's my name) raptly
seeks as its Center,
follows as its Star?
(The Divine Narcissus, vv. 86-111. See also vv. 2079-98 and 1241-44)

Nature glorifies God and gives Beauty back.

The order of nature does not stand by itself but has a relation to grace that has changed several times in the past. In the beginning nature and grace were wedded so that nature was benign, but the devil trapped man into offending God and many special graces were removed.

This separation of grace and nature caused man to be unhappy, reduced him to misery, and caused nature to cease being benign. There was, for example, the Deluge *(The Divine Narcissus,* vv. 472-74).

God is not a passive witness to nature and its relation with grace. He can if He will arrest the operations of nature or go beyond them, as He did when He brought about the virgin birth *(The Divine Narcissus,* 1008-10). God also refused to admit the separation of grace and nature in the instance of the Immaculate Conception, which is alluded to when Narcissus looks into the fountain (Mary) and marvels at the untarnished beauty there (vv. 1326-95). God also takes exception to nature when he allows miracles. In the sacramental play *Joseph's Scepter* there is a miracle above nature when the boy Joseph foretells the future fat and lean years of Egypt. No natural knowledge can account for this prophecy, which is made possible only by special grace.

Sor Juana may have exalted nature in *The Dream* and a few other passages of her works, but her verses constantly show that for her nature comes from the Hand of God and imposes order. This is the nature of the Scholastics.

CHAPTER 6

The Alleged Mysticism of Sor Juana[1]

IN Chapter 1 we saw that a black legend has grown about Sor Juana, by which she is pictured as a clever, scheming woman who deceived the ecclesiastical society of her day. Such a picture is misleading. Sor Juana was an ordinary nun endowed with an extraordinary intellect. A person so endowed, it seems, is bound to make enemies.

In addition to the black legend, a mystical story has also grown around Sor Juana. I call it a story since it has not quite enjoyed the wider reception of a legend. Amado Nervo (1870-1919), one of Mexico's most famous poets, spoke of Sor Juana's "mystical poetry." Ezequiel Chávez, whose long *Essay on the Psychology of Sor Juana* (1931) may itself be justly called an intuitive, quasimystical effort, said that the highest goal of Sor Juana was "the development of her mysticism." And Alfonso Méndez Plancarte accepted the thesis of Chávez.[2]

The argument of Méndez Plancarte in the second volume of his edition of Sor Juana's complete works is the strongest argument that has been made for her mysticism. First he says that only God knows whether she became a mystic: "es el secreto del Rey" . . . (Tob., XII, 7). Having made this qualification, he says: "Moreover, once we modify even slightly that most technical interpretation of the word 'mystic,' we can on certain evidence speak of her 'mystical soul,' which Don Ezequiel Chávez has already detected with great insight." To support this opinion, Méndez Plancarte offers the following evidence: three rather long poems *(romances)* and three short passages from her sacramental plays. He also refers in passing to some of her other poems *(letras)* and some contemplative prose works, though he neither quotes them nor bases any argument on them.

Before discussing the argument of Méndez Plancarte, it would be well to say something about mysticism as a phenomenon in literature. The reader should bear in mind that this chapter is not so much concerned with mystical theology as with the signposts a mystic leaves in his writings. If these signposts are discovered, the question may later be asked: Did Sor Juana leave them in her prose and poetry?

I *The Signposts of Mystical Literature*

In the first place, mystical literature is based on experience. The mystic does not write about what ought to be or might have been, but about things that he heard and touched and saw, if not with the senses of the body, then with the eyes of the soul: "and I say it because I know it through experience"; "I will say nothing that I have not experienced a great deal"; "the Lord said to me"; "but I will tell what happened to me." (See St. Theresa of Avila, *Libro de la vida,* in *Obras completas,* BAC, Madrid 1951, pp. 657, 695, 723, 808. These few phrases are taken at random; there are literally hundreds more like them.) St. Theresa writes about her experience with God and the devil, who often tries to thwart her union with God, in much the same way another person would write about his experience in the world and at home. With this difference: she has unusual energy.

It should be noted that the personal experience of the mystic is habitual, which doesn't mean that he is in a constant cloud and out of touch with reality—he may be the practical reformer of a religious order—but means that the mystical state requires a long period of preparation and, once arrived at, endures intermittently until death. That the life and work of St. John of the Cross confirm this habitualness can be seen in the well-documented biography of Padre Crisógono. Perhaps the following testimony of a contemporary of St. John, one of many such testimonies, refers to the night on which he left his cares forgotten among the lilies:

Father John the Evangelist, who was then in this monastery of Segovia, told this witness that many nights all night long he saw Friar John of the Cross at the window of his cell, from where one could see the sky and countryside, in prayer; and so much inflamed, absorbed, and carried away in God, that, although he tugged at the Saint, he could not bring him around, and seeing him thus, he stayed with him until morning or until he came to himself, and then the Saint said to him: What are you doing here? or Why have you come? (The Declaration of Mother María of the Conception.)[3]

The first signpost of mystical literature is *habitual experience.*

A second characteristic of mystical literature is the recurrence of certain metaphors and images, which the French critic Gaston Etchegoyen called a *traditional terminology.*[4] Since the mystic is trying to communicate the experiences of an impalpable relationship (impalpable for the reader), he must use words that are concrete and known to all, and have at the same time spiritual connotations. The two most frequent images are fire with all its corollaries: light, flame, sun; and water with its corollaries: ocean, river, fountain, rain. Thus, in his exegesis of the "active night of the senses," St. John speaks of the dazzling *(encandilamiento)* of the appetite, an excessive light that a man must get rid of before he can arrive at the dark night of the soul. St. Theresa repeatedly uses the fire metaphor. And in Raymond Lull, it appears in the *Book of the Lover and the Loved One.* As for water, the crystal fountain of St. John is the Faith; and St. Theresa uses water to describe as best she can her four grades of prayer.

The Song of Songs is one of the basic sources of the traditional terminology; for example, the Bridegroom and the Bride. And there are many other usages, too numerous to be more than mentioned here: path, footstep, Lover, Beloved; the reader comes across constant repetition of words and ideas such as sighs, flood of tears, tears, love, fire, fountain, the crazy one—all of these in Raymond Lull; experience, visions, I do not know how, nothing nothing, devil, look look, a worm so vile, believe believe, many many, garden, fountain, death, life—all of these in St. Theresa; happy fortune, night, the Beloved, the theft you stole, solitude, transcending all knowledge—all of these in St. John of the Cross; and so insistent is this repetition that the mystics appear at times to be amorous, breathless hammerers who are so anxious to convey their message that they will hit it, hit it, hit it, until something like a huge magnetic field is set up in which the reader will find his place without any self-effort. There is also in the mystics a superabundance of exclamations and interrogations by which they somehow hope to express intuitive experiences that cannot be adequately expressed in the ordinary discursive language of human beings.

The following, then, are to be found in the traditional terminology: fire, water, the path, the footstep, the Song of Songs with its erotic language, and a peculiar kind of exclamatory repetition.

Another trait of mystical literature is its paradoxicalness, which arises from the disproportion between the Lover (the mystic) and the Object of his love (God) or comes, like the exclamations above, from the hiatus between intuitive experience and man's discursive language. There are different kinds of paradoxes: the Lover complaining, or even quarreling, with the Loved One, and the unusual attitude that considers pain, suffering, tribulation, and joy, happiness, love to be all one and the same thing. But the greatest paradox is the "I don't know" (*yo no sé*) which is the most striking phrase of St. Theresa in the *Libro de la vida* (*Book of Her Life*); the verse "an I don't know what that stays stammering" (*un no sé qué que queda balbuciendo*) is one of the memorable ones of St. John's; and Raymond Lull was so eager to bridge the gap between the human and the divine that he claimed to be able to prove articles of faith. How? In his absence the reader must answer for him: I don't know (*Yo no sé*).[5]

The last characteristic of mystical literature is the most difficult to describe. Just as the average opera fan knows a good performance when he sees one without being able to write a treatise on the subject, so the untutored reader of the mystics knows the genuine fruits of mysticism when he comes upon them; he can't define them exactly, but they are there. Mystical literature has a certain unmistakable flavor, which comes from the sensible signs of Love that always accompany it: *Insouciance, Confiance, Souffrances*.[6]

Habitual experience, traditional terminology, paradox, *confiance* (overflowing hope): where are these signposts in the prose and poetry of Sor Juana Inés de la Cruz? Apparently, nowhere.

II *The Evidence: Sor Juana's Literature*

There is a strong autobiographical evidence against Sor Juana's being a mystic. She has left *The Reply to Sor Filotea*, a "book of her life," in which there is not the least hint of St. Theresa's raptures, visions, revelations, "I don't know," modes of prayer, and art of loving. On the contrary, Sor Juana tells her reader she has many intellectual interests that are plainly non-mystical; for example, in one passage of *The Reply to Sor Filotea* she tells why she likes to study so much:

I do not study in order to write, and much less to teach, which would be a disproportionate pride in me, but only so that by studying I shall be less ignorant. That is the way I answer, and that is the way I feel.

These lines do not come from the pen of a mystic.

If the standards of habitual experience, the traditional terminology, the paradox, and *confiance* are accepted, it is difficult to see how one can apply the term "mystical" to Sor Juana's three sacramental plays with their *loas*, her *loas* on the king's birthday, all the *villancicos* for the feast days of the Blessed Virgin and the saints, the play *The Trials of a Noble House, The Reply to Sor Filotea*, the poems to the Marqueses de la Laguna, the courtly poems, the Latin poems, the sonnets to Fabio, the epistolary verses, and other like poetry. The reader never encounters the crazy one, the fool of love, the anxious search of the Bride for the Bridegroom, the dark night of the soul, and the "it happened to me." Many of Sor Juana's writings were religious because they were prompted by the liturgy of the Church (for example, the *villancicos* of 1676, 1677, 1679, 1685, 1689, and 1690); however, Christian literature is not necessarily mystical literature. Perhaps the fact that most of Sor Juana's works are Christian has led her critics to call her a mystic.[7]

Méndez Plancarte saw evidence of mysticism in several parts of Sor Juana's poetry. In Volume II of his edition of Sor Juana's complete works, he says:

Even among these poems which were meant to be sung, some of that might be glimpsed, for example, in the Poems on the Profession of a Nun, or in some of those poems on St. Bernard—the eucharistic poems —so pleasing several of them to Mother Castillo, the mystical Clarisa de Tunja, that she did not disdain adding some of her own stanzas to them. And if we take in all Sor Juana's writings, certain passages of her Contemplative Prose inspire in us an even more sacred respect;

her sacramental plays do the same, but above all are the three poems
(*romances*) called: "Sweet lover of the soul . . .," "I have in me a
great care . . .," and "While Grace doth stir me . . ." And when we
look into her sacramental plays, the imprisonment of the royal martyr
Hermenegildo certainly throws light on the happiness to be found in
detachment and the joy in tribulation:

> All is from God, nothing is mine;
> His will be done!
>
> .   .   .   .
>
> What comfort I take in you
> seeing myself of all divested!
>
> .   .   .   .
>
> Rather I have been happy
> in losing all for you!

In *The Divine Narcissus* not only does the passionate rapture of Christ
the Beautiful shine forth in the most exquisite and famous passages,
but there are other tremulous suggestions of secret intimacy:

> My heart within
> my breast seems
> softened wax
> near the ardent soul.

The reader must consider these thoughts of Méndez Plancarte.
As for the words of St. Hermenegildo, they are not mystical, but
part of the narrative poetry of this historical sacramental play.
At the end of the first scene, St. Leander advises Hermenegildo
concerning the excellence of making sacrifices for God. Hermenegildo answers Leander, thanks him, and concludes by saying:
"All is from God, nothing is mine:/ His will be done!"

At the beginning of the fourth scene, Hermenegildo is presented
in chains. He has a soliloquy in which he addresses this longed-
for prison where the chains are glories rather than afflictions, and
then he says to this prison: "What comfort I take in you,/ seeing
myself of all divested . . ." He goes on to recount his past
possessions in this world, the scepter, the royal purple, and
others, after which he says: "as long as all is lost for You, there
is no pain: Rather I have been happy in losing all for You!"
Isolated passages such as these, falling within the narrative con-
text of the play, should not be interpreted as mystical. The same

criticism may be made of the verses "My heart within my breast
. . . ," which are the words of the allegorical figure Human
Nature after the death of the divine Narcissus, Christ. None of
these passages is a personal experience.

The Poems on the Profession of a Nun consist of four *letras,*
each with a short refrain and couplets of somewhat more than
twenty lines. The *letras* create the atmosphere of a pastoral
wedding in which a young shepherdess is being married to a
very great Lord, who condescends to become a shepherd and
puts on rustic garments for the marriage feast. The virgin
bride is very happy on this her wedding day, and a unique
day it is since the vows of marriage will leave the bride's
virginity intact (a nun is married to Christ) and the bridegroom
is of such an exacting disposition that "not even for hearing Mass/
will he let her leave the house." All are invited to share in this
joyous occasion: "Young shepherds of the town/ come to see
a Wedding,/ Come to the feast, come señores,/ today a girl is
married, and it is for love!/ Come, fly, winged Seraphim!"

These *letras* do not bear any suggestions of mysticism; they
are rather an adaptation of the popular songs to a special occasion
that is at once religious and social. The general style of the
letras calls to mind one of those pastoral scenes from a play of
Lope de Vega rather than the peculiar pastoral poetry of St.
John of the Cross. Though it is true that in these *letras* Sor Juana
uses expressions such as Bride, Bridegroom, Lover, and a few
others that might be mistaken for the traditional terminology,
these expressions are by no means used mystically. In seventeenth-
century Mexico it must have been a commonplace to call a nun
the bride of Christ.

The works of Sor Juana that most resemble mystical literature
are the three poems *(romances)* mentioned by Méndez Plancarte
"Sweet lover of the soul . . ." "I have in me a great care . . . ,"
and "While Grace doth stir me . . . ,"; the greatest semblance is
to be found in "I have in me a great care." Here are selections
from this poem, in English:

1. I have in me a great care
2. and so shy, I believe
3. though I know I feel it so much,
4. even I myself do not feel it.

13. If it is licit, even owed,
14. this tenderness I feel,
15. why must they reprove me
16. if I pay that which I owe?
37. Whosoever hears this will say,
38. if it is so why do I sorrow?
39. But my anxious heart will say
40. for that very reason.
57. Who so penetrates the recesses
58. of my heart has seen
59. that I myself am forming
60. my dolorous woe
65. I die—who will believe it?—at the hand
66. of what I love most,
67. and the reason for my death
68. is the love I bear it
69. And so nourishing, sadly,
70. my life with the venom,
71. the very death I live
72. is the life with which I die.

This *romance* has several verses that are suggestive of mysticism: the *yo no sé* ("I don't know") in verses 3 and 4, the paradoxical use of sorrow *(peno)* and dolorous woe *(dolores)* in verses 38 and 60, the confusion of love and pain in verses 67 and 68, and the idea of I die because I do not die *(muero porque no muero)* in the next to the last stanza; moreover, the poem as a whole concerns the amorous relationship of God and the author. But the verses are not lyrical and are far too conceptual to be considered the ecstatic writing down of a mystical experience. The soul does not act as if alone with God; the line "why must they reprove me?" (v. 15) does not belong in a mystical poem; either it comes from one of the literary fashions of Sor Juana's day—apparent oppositions, paradoxes, antitheses, and contradictions, all of which abound in her verses—or it is another instance of the protest she so often makes against those who will not leave her to the solitude of her convent; indeed, this protest itself seems to be a literary fashion with her. There are other verses that also preclude the solitude of the Lover and the Beloved: line 37, "whosoever hears this will say"; line 41, "Oh our human weakness"; line 46, "the desire we have to be loved";

and line 57, "Who so penetrates the recesses." These verses do not have the ring of personal experience.

Some of the stanzas that seem to carry the traditional terminology are more conventional than spontaneous; for example, the first four lines: "I have in me a great care/ and so shy, I believe/ though I know I feel it so much,/ even I myself do not feel it." These lines may resemble the mystical "I do not know" (*yo no sé*) but if the reader looks at the opening verses of one of Sor Juana's secular poems, her *redondillas*, he will find:

> This amorous torment,
> implanted in my heart,
> I know I feel it, but I know not
> the reason why I feel it.

Furthermore, Sor Juana's "the very death I live/ is the life with which I die" (vv. 71-72, above) may resemble the ineffable paradox of the mystic, but the reader who examines the poem carefully will see that this *death-life* comes at the end of a long series of antitheses that begins with the "I know I feel it, but I know not/ the reason why I feel it" just quoted.

The criticism that has been made of the poem "I have in me a great care" also holds for the other poems, "While Grace doth stir me," and "Sweet lover of the soul." These poems may be called religious verse, but they are not to be taken for the lyrical expressions of a mystic.

To sum up this chapter on the alleged mysticism of Sor Juana, her writings do not show the signposts of mystical literature: habitual experience, the traditional terminology, paradoxicalness, *confiance*. Occasionally she uses words that belong to the traditional terminology, but their use is wooden; and the paradoxes that exist in her verses belong to the intellectual conceits of the seventeenth century rather than to the language of the Lover trying vainly to describe the experience with the Beloved. There is never the rapture, the ineffability of the *confiance*.

CHAPTER 7

Conclusion

SOR Juana Inés de la Cruz (1648-1695) lived and wrote during the reign of Charles II, when Spanish literature was on the decline. The writings and manners of the time were marked by a rather severe imitation: in Mexico, just as the viceroy's court was an imitation of the King's court in Spain, so poems and plays were an imitation of the works of the great authors of the peninsula, Góngora and Calderón. In the case of Sor Juana, Calderón in particular was the master and she the student, his most competent student in the New World. Thus, her theater and poetry belong really to Spanish peninsular literature rather than American literature; there was nothing distinctly American about them.

Sor Juana was, in modern parlance, an intellectual. In *The Reply to Sor Filotea* she discusses some arguments she has made against the famous orator of the seventeenth century, the Portuguese Jesuit, Vieyra. She says she has been sharply criticized for opposing Vieyra and she resents this, for "just as I was free to disagree with Vieyra, so others are free to disagree with my judgment." Sor Juana's insistence on intellectual freedom is characteristic of her thought.

The criticism of Sor Juana has been extremely irregular. She was neither the mystic nor the irreligious schemer that some critics have taken her to be. She was rather a seventeenth-century nun who found time in the middle of her religious exercises to write memorable works such as *The Dream, The Trials of a Noble House, The Divine Narcissus, The Reply to Sor Filotea,* and a score or more of good poems. She also wrote many mediocre carols and poems for occasions of Church and State.

In the twilight age of an old Europe, Sor Juana represented the harmony of faith and reason. She had an unusual desire to know but she always tempered this desire with love. Her last acts reveal her true character: she insisted on helping her companions during a plague, and this brought about her death.

Notes and References

Chapter One

1. Ludwig Pfandl, *Die Zehnte Muse von Mexico* (Munchen, 1946). The Spanish translation of this book appeared in 1963.

2. For example, compare Sor Juana's *gracioso* (figure of fun) with Calderón's. See Charles David Ley, *El gracioso en el teatro de la península* (Madrid, 1954).

3. See José María de Cossío, "Observaciones sobre la vida y la obra de Sor Juana Inés de la Cruz," in the *Homenaje a Sor Juana Inés de la Cruz* of the Real Academia Española (Madrid, 1952), pp. 18-20.

4. See Ermilo Abréu Gómez, prologue, *Poesías de Sor Juana* (México, 1940); Clara Campoamor, *Sor Juana* (Buenos Aires, 1943); Elizabeth Wallace, *Sor Juana* (México, 1944); and Anita Arroyo, *Razón y pasión de Sor Juana* (Mexico, 1952). See also the newspaper article of Alfonso Méndez Plancarte, "Sor Juana heterodoxa, histérica y otros piropos," in the newspaper *El Universal* (Mexico, May 21, 1945).

5. See José María Pemán, "Sinceridad y artificio en la poesía de Sor Juana Inés de la Cruz," in the *Homenaje a Sor Juana Inés de la Cruz* of the Real Academia Española (Madrid, 1952), pp. 31-32.

6. See Antonio de Robles, *Diario de sucesos notables*, Tomo I (México, 1946), 3-14.

7. Alfonso Méndez Plancarte, *Obras completas de Sor Juana* (México, 1951), Vol. I, xxviii.

8. From the biography by Padre Calleja, as quoted by Méndez Plancarte, *Obras completas*, Vol. I, xxviii.

9. See Ludwig Pfandl, *Sor Juana Inés de la Cruz* (México, 1963), pp. 47-48.

10. According to Ezequiel Chávez. As Antonio Castro Leal has pointed out, Chávez did not mention his source. See Sor Juana Inés de la Cruz, *Poesía, teatro y prosa*, edición y prólogo de Antonio Castro Leal (México, 1965), p. xxviii.

11. Miss Dorothy Schons has argued that these "four thousand volumes" should read "four hundred." See Méndez Plancarte, *Obras completas*, Vol. I, lxi. If Sor Juana had four thousand volumes, she

had the best library in all of Spanish America: see Castro Leal, *loc. cit.* (note 10, above).

12. But see Ludwig Pfandl, *Sor Juana Inés de la Cruz,* p. 76.

13. See the opinion of Alberto G. Salceda in the *Obras completas de Sor Juana,* Vol. IV, xliii. Salceda edited the fourth and last volume of Sor Juana's *Obras completas* after the death of Alfonso Méndez Plancarte.

14. In *The Reply to Sor Filotea* Sor Juana does not mention her childhood friends, the games she played, trips she took, and similar experiences. To be sure, *The Reply,* is an intellectual autobiography and an apology for learning, but the reader can only regret she has not told more about her everyday life.

15. According to Sor Juana, all the sciences are linked and the comprehension of one helps the comprehension of another. She speaks of a "universal chain," which falls within the traditional idea of the great chain of being. See Arthur O. Lovejoy, *The Great Chain of Being* (Cambridge, Massachusetts, 1936).

16. Sor Juana's problem in *The Reply to Sor Filotea* has always existed and exists today. It is the question of revelation and reason. Should there be a primacy of revelation? A primacy of reason? Or a harmony of revelation and reason? Before reading *The Reply to Sor Filotea,* the reader should consult Étienne Gilson's *Reason and Revelation in the Middle Ages* (New York, 1938).

17. See José María de Cossío, "Observaciones sobre la vida y la obra de Sor Juana Inés de la Cruz," in the *Homenaje a Sor Juana Inés de la Cruz* of the Real Academia Española (Madrid, 1952).

Chapter Two

1. Ludwig Pfandl misinterpreted this verse in his prose translation of *The Dream.* Sor Juana wrote that man is a "compendium who absolute/ is like the Angel, the plant, the beast;/ whose haughty baseness/ all Nature participated in./ Why? Because perhaps more fortunate/ than all, man/ would be elevated / thanks to an amorous union" (vv. 692-99). Pfandl translated "amorous union" as "the amorous couch." See the edition of the *Primero sueño* of the Universidad de Buenos Aires, Facultad de Filosofía y Letras (Buenos Aires, 1953), pp. 21-31.

2. See R. P. Sertillanges, *La philosophie de St. Thomas D'Aquin* (Paris, 1940), I, 68. And see Jacques Maritain, *Éléments de philosophie,* I, *Introduction générale à la philosophie* (Paris 1951), 124: "the school of Aristotle and of St. Thomas teach that ideas differ essentially from sensations and images, but they are drawn from sensations and images by the activity of the spiritual light that is in us."

3. See Karl Vossler's essay "El mundo en el sueño," in Sor Juana Inés de la Cruz, *Primero sueño* (Buenos Aires, 1953), p. 12.

4. Alfonso Méndez Plancarte explains all the mythological references in his prose translation of *The Dream*. See volume I of his *Obras completas de Sor Juana*, or his edition of *El sueño* for the *Textos de literatura mexicana* (México, 1951).

5. Here is a sign of Luis de Góngora's influence in *The Dream*, the formula "A, if not B." Sometimes A and B are really in opposition to one another, sometimes they are two alternatives, and sometimes they are no more than a repetition since A and B are apt to be synonyms. In the verse "which she extinguishes if she does not desecrate," Sor Juana offers A and B as two alternatives. See Dámaso Alonso, *La lengua poética de Góngora* (Madrid, 1950), p. 138 ff.

6. See Pedro Salinas, *Reality and the Poet in Spanish Poetry* (Baltimore, 1940), pp. 131-47.

7. Salinas, *op. cit.*, p. 146: "Góngora would never call bread bread or wine wine. His poetic system is the opposite of this."

8. Sor Juana's order brings to mind the words of Segismund in Calderón's *Life Is A Dream* (vv. 103-72) which appeared in 1635: "what God has given a stream, a fish, a beast, a bird." But her poetic purpose is different than Calderón's since she does not have to get on with a dramatic action. She does not have to keep her thought within Calderon's highly regular strophe, the *décima*, but can wander more freely in the *silva* she has chosen for her poem.

9. See Tomás Navarro Tomás, *Arte del verso*, 4th ed. (México, 1968), p. 165.

10. Apparently Sor Juana took this line from Góngora's *Polifemo*, octava 22: "Mudo la noche el can, el día dormido/ de cerro en cerro y sombra en sombra yace." See Méndez Plancarte, *Obras completas de Sor Juana*, Vol. I, 584.

11. See Marcelino Menéndez y Pelayo, *Historia de la poesía hispanoamericana*, Vol. I (Santander, 1948), 75. Had Menéndez y Pelayo belonged to a younger generation or had he lived longer, he might have changed his opinion—see Dámaso Alonso, *Las palinodias de Don Marcelino* (Madrid, 1956), p. 13.

12. See *Hispania*, Vol. XLIII (December, 1960), 519, note 1; and *Hispanic Review*, Vol. XXVIII (1960), 234, note 3.

13. See Ludwig Pfandl, "Sor Juana como soñadora," in the *Primero sueño* (Buenos Aires, 1953), p. 23.

14. See Karl Vossler, "El mundo en el sueño," in *Primero sueño* (Buenos Aires, 1953), p. 12.

Chapter Three

1. Francisco Monterde interprets the unity of the *festejo* in a

112 SOR JUANA INÉS DE LA CRUZ

different manner. "Poseemos . . . un programa completo de teatro barroco mexicano. . . . Al hablar del barroco mexicano se piensa en aquellos motivos churriguerescos en los cuales, en torno de las flores y frutos más destacados por el tallista, se agrupan otros frutos y otras flores. Así acontece en tal programa barroco, en el que lo saliente está constituido por las tres jornadas de la comedia. Pero antes de la jornada inicial, se desliza el entorchado de la loa que va seguida de la primera canción; después de la última jornada, aun pasea su cuadriga el 'sarao,' y entre jornada y jornada, además de la segunda canción, trenzan sus diálogos—frutos morenos—dos sainetes." See Francisco Monterde, *Cultura mexicana. Aspectos literarios* (México, 1946), pp. 56-57.

2. See *The Trials of a Noble House*, Act I, v. 589. And see Charles David Ley, *El gracioso en el teatro de la península* (Madrid, 1954), p. 212: "For Calderón, society is made, and well bound, with steel walls. The servant was born and raised to be a servant, and nothing else. There is nothing in Calderón's *gracioso*, none of the vague aspirations and ancestry that Lope de Vega gave to the figure."

3. Hymen is the god of marriage.

4. See Arthur O. Lovejoy, *The Great Chain of Being* (Cambridge, Massachusetts, 1936).

5. Acevedo was probably the playwright Don Francisco de Acevedo. See Francisco Monterde's *Cultura mexicana. Aspectos literarios,* (México, 1946), pp. 56-57, and Alberto Salceda's introduction to Volume IV of the *Obras completas de Sor Juana*, xxviii.

6. Don Fernando Deza was a public official in whose house *The Trials of a Noble House* was staged. Muñiz, who is referred to in the *sainete* as Andrés, was probably another official, the Alférez Andrés Muñiz. See Monterde and Salceda, note 4 above.

7. There are several obscure literary references and untranslatable puns in the *sainete*. According to A. Salceda, Sor Juana is alluding here to a poem Góngora dedicated to a famous lady whose father was the Señor de Zuheros: "¡Cuántos silbos, cuántas voces/la Nava oyó de Zuheros." Some of the puns are based on the Castilian and Mexican ways of pronouncing the letter *z*.

8. His utterance "I die" ("Muerto quedo") is another serious line that is generally spoken by a nobleman in a play such as *None Except the King* by Rojas Zorrilla, but it is ridiculous when placed alongside "Hisses the first time out?" ("¿Al primer tapón silbos?").

9. Pedro Calderón de la Barca, *Los flatos,* in *Las comedias de Calderón* (Biblioteca de autores españoles: Madrid, 1926), Tomo XIV, 641. Emilio Cotarelo y Mori describes the *mojiganga* in Volume I of his *Colección de entremeses, loas, bailes, jácaras y mojigangas desde fines del siglo XVI a mediados del XVIII* (Madrid, 1911).

10. See Francisco Monterde's *Cultura mexicana* (México, 1946), p. 89. He speaks of a "labor de autocritica."

11. A study of this political philosophy would make an interesting monograph. Consider, for example, the application of Aristotle's theory of natural slavery to the American Indian: "The most startling argument developed at Valladolid, certainly the most vigorously disputed then and now, was the second justification propounded by Sepúlveda for the Spaniards' overlordship: the 'natural rudeness and inferiority' of the Indians which, he declared unequivocally, accorded with the doctrine of the philosophers that some men are born to be natural slaves." Lewis Hanke, *Aristotle and the American Indians* (Chicago, 1959), p. 44.

12. Almost all of Sor Juana's sources are ancient Latin, medieval Latin, or Spanish. There is no evidence of a direct French source, and so it is better to emphasize Cicero rather than Montaigne.

'13. *Obras de Lope de Vega.* Publicadas por la Real Academia Española (Madrid, 1896), Tomo VI, 128, column 1.

Chapter Four

1. Alfonso Méndez Plancarte makes an interesting comment in his notes: "The fact that Fallen Angelic Nature willed to be the 'bride of Narcissus' (v. 85) might refer to the opinion of Suárez *(De Angelis*, lib. VII, c. 13) that Lucifer's sin was a disordinate desire for the Hypostatic Union and his refusal to adore the Incarnate Word if God were to grant human nature such a high state, which he, Lucifer, would never attain. See vv. 648-654." See the *Obras completas de Sor Juana*, Vol. III, 520.

2. The sacramental plays used moveable scenery mounted on wheels, and this ensemble was called a *carro* or cart. Many plays required four or five carts. The reader might look at Cervantes' *Don Quixote*, Second Part (1615), Chapter 11.

3. See Méndez Plancarte, Vol. III, 540 and his references to the New Testament: Mark IX, 16-24 and Matthew IX, 32-33.

4. Méndez Plancarte, who is the most outstanding *sorjuanista* (Sor Juana critic), has the unfortunate tendency of comparing Sor Juana and Calderón, at the expense of Calderón. One example of this comparison is the earthquake of verse 1706, which he compares with the earthquake Calderón uses in his *comedia, Echo and Narcissus;* he speak of "a cheap theatrical effect" in Calderón. See Méndez Plancarte, Vol. III, 545.

In the first place, a critic should draw a comparison between two sacramental plays and not between a sacramental play and a regular play *(comedia).* Certainly the earthquake of Calderón's sacramental play *Life Is a Dream* (v. 1214) is as relevant to the play as Sor Juana's earthquake in *The Divine Narcissus*. Secondly, and this refers to Méndez Plancarte's general tendency to belittle Calderón, there is no need to lessen that playwright's stature in order to add to Sor Juana's. He is always the master and she a competent disciple.

5. See the articles on *Auto* and *Carro* in the *Diccionario de literatura española*, 2a. ed. (Madrid, 1953).

6. See the *Biblioteca de autores españoles*, Tomo IX, *Comedias de Calderón*, 586, column 1.

7. *Comedias de Calderón*, p. 579, column 1; p. 586, column 1. Sor Juana, *The Divine Narcissus*, vv. 775-78. Concerning the verses called *ecos*, see Calderón, p. 291, column 1, and *The Divine Narcissus*, vv. 1480-1691.

8. Literally, "God of Seeds" *(Dios de las Semillas)*. For the identity of this Aztec god see Méndez Plancarte's well-documented notes, Vol. III, 503-4.

9. In her article "Some Obscure Points in the Life of Sor Juana Inés de la Cruz" *(Modern Philology*, Nov. 1926, pp. 141-62) Miss Dorothy Schons says that Sor Juana's books, especially her theater, were published in Spain because conditions were less severe there. According to Miss Schons, the Archbishop Aguiar y Seixas was a fanatic who especially attacked the theater.

10. See the notes of Alfonso Méndez Plancarte, *(Obras completas*, Vol. III, 564-67), who traces the historical argument of Sor Juana in Mariana's *Historia de España*, 1601. And see the articles on the Visigoths and Hermenegildo in the *Diccionario de historia de España*, 2 vols. (Madrid, 1952).

11. See the series *Clásicos castellanos*, No. 69: Calderón de la Barca, *Autos sacramentales* I (Madrid, 1951), xiv-xxiii.

12. Méndez Plancarte's notes to vv. 1815-94 correct a theological error of Sor Juana. In her play Hermenegildo denies the validity of the sacrament consecrated by the Arian, but Méndez Plancarte points out that the sacrament is valid if the Holy Orders are valid. Although Hermenegildo should not accept Arianism, he should not deny the consecratory powers of its bishops. [According to the heresy known as Donatism, the validity of a sacrament depends upon the state of grace of the priest or bishop who administers it.]

Chapter Five

1. The famous critic Marcelino Menéndez Pelayo (1856-1912) took a dim view of Sor Juana's *villancicos*. See his *Historia de la poesía hispanoamericana* (Santander, 1948), Vol. I, 68-69.

Méndez Plancarte *(Obras completas de Sor Juana*, Vol. II, 363) gives examples of Negro poetry in the Spanish authors Góngora, Calderón, and Manuel León Marchante.

2. See Albert A. Sicroff, *Les Controverses Des Statuts De "Pureté De Sang" En Espagne Du XVe Au XVIIe Siècle* (Paris, 1960). The Spaniards contradicted themselves with their idea of purity of blood, which really called for purity of doctrine. Of two full brothers one might have the so-called purity of blood and the other not have it; for example, one might be an orthodox Catholic and the other a heretic or a *penitenciado* (a heretic who returned to the Church did not have *limpieza de sangre*.)

3. The reader should weigh a problem that Méndez Plancarte has raised in his study: are the *villancicos* to be considered part of the drama or not? Several critics have suggested they are part of dramatic literature, namely, Pedro Henríquez Ureña, Carolina Michaelis, Ezequiel Chávez. But Méndez Plancarte has the last word when he says: [It is] "a delightful idea, but contrary to the facts, since everything was sung from the Choir, the "Chapel" or Orpheon of the churches, without anything that even remotely resembled theatrical decoration, dress and action . . . every dialogue is more or less capable of being dramatized (as some *villancicos* are), but this does not mean in any way that we are now "within the limits of dramatic literature." *(Obras completas de Sor Juana,* Vol. II, lii.)

4. Calderón referred to this hierarchy when he wrote: "and there is no/animal, plant, or stone/ that does not have/ a determined quality." *(Life Is a Dream,* Act II, W. 1008-11). He also has Death say in a sacramental play: "and of God's judgment a fatal flash / am I, who prostrates before my fury / the vegetable, the sensitive, the rational." *(The Supper of King Baltasar,* vv. 668-71). This does not mean that Sor Juana borrowed the philosophy from Calderón. It was rather the predominant philosophy of seventeenth-century Spain and Mexico.

5. In English literature, one of the best expressions of this idea is by Gerard Manley Hopkins:

THE LEADEN ECHO

How to keep—is there any, is there none such, nowhere known some,
bow or brooch or braid or brace, lace, latch or catch or key to keep
Back beauty, keep it, beauty, beauty, beauty, . . . from vanishing away?

THE GOLDEN ECHO

Spare!
There is one, yes I have one (Hush there!);
Only not within seeing of the sun,

.   .   .   .

Give beauty back, beauty, beauty, beauty, back to God beauty's self
and beauty's giver.
See; not a hair is, not an eyelash, no the least lash lost; every hair
  Is, hair of the head, numbered." (See "The Leaden Echo and

The Golden Echo," *Poems of Gerard Manley Hopkins* (Oxford University Press, 1948).

Chapter Six

1. This chapter originally appeared as an article in *Hispanic Review*, XXVIII (1960), 233-44.

2. On the other hand, Ermilo Abreu Gómez, Elizabeth Wallace, Karl Vossler, and José María Pemán deny that Sor Juana was a mystic. Abreu Gómez makes the strongest denial, for he maintains that she was not even religious, let alone mystical. See the following books: E. Chávez, *Ensayo de psicología de Sor Juana* (Barcelona, 1931); E. Abreu Gómez, *Poesías de Juana Inés de la Cruz* (Mexico, 1940); E. Wallace, *Sor Juana Inés de la Cruz, Poetisa de corte y convento* (Mexico, 1944); Karl Vossler, "La Décima Musa de México," in *Obras escogidas de Sor Juana* (Buenos Aires, 1946), pp. 9-45; J. M. Pemán, "Sinceridad y artificio en la poesía de Sor Juana Inés de la Cruz," in *Homenaje a Sor Juana . . . de la Real Academia Española* (Madrid, 1952), pp. 31-48.

3. See the *Vida de San Juan de la Cruz*, p. 412, note 18; in *Vida y obra de San Juan de la Cruz*, (BAC: Madrid, 1940). In his book on St. Bernard of Clairvaux, Etienne Gilson speaks of the *vicissitudo* in mysticism, which he defines as "Alternate presences and absences of the Bridegroom, due to the fact that the soul is united to a non-glorified body." The state of ecstasy is itself fleeting, but the *vicissitudo* can be called habitual. See Gilson, *Mystical Theology of St. Bernard* (New York, 1940), p. 241.

4. G. Etchegoyen, *L'amour divin. Essai sur les sources de Sainte Thérèse* (Bordeaux, 1923), p. 31.

5. R. Menéndez Pidal explains the reason for paradoxical language in "Las imágenes y la experiencia psicológica en el lenguaje teresiano," *La Lengua de Cristóbal Colón*, 2a. ed. (Col. Austral: Buenos Aires, 1944), p. 83.

6. See Etchegoyen, pp. 180-84. Etchegoyen adds *nostalgie* to the other three. The author of the present chapter included this *nostalgie* in his article of 1960 (see note 1), but he has omitted it here since he no longer feels that it applies to the mystics.

Concerning *confiance*, consider these words of Gilson (p. 24) on St. Bernard: "For there, where charity reigns, there at the same time is full confidence in the issue of the Day of Judgment. This fiducia, offspring of charity, is an essential factor in St. Bernard's doctrine."

7. Menéndez Pelayo makes a careful distinction between Christian and mystical literature in his *De la poesía mística* (1881). In *San Isidro, Cervantes y otros estudios*, 2a. ed. (Col. Austral: Buenos Aires, 1944).

Selected Bibliography

PRIMARY SOURCES

1. Editions of Sor Juana's Works

Antología. Edición de Elias L. Rivers (Salamanca-Madrid-Barcelona: Biblioteca Anaya, 1965).

Los empeños de una casa. Edición y prólogo de J. Jiménez Rueda (México: Ed. de la Universidad Nacional Autónoma, 1952).

Obras escogidas. (Buenos Aires: Colección Austral, 1946).

Obras completas. 4 volumes, edición de Alfonso Méndez Plancarte y Alberto G. Salceda (México: Fondo de Cultura Económica, 1951-1957).

Poesías. Edición, prólogo y notas de E. Abreu Gómez, 2a. ed. (México: Ediciones Botas, 1948).

Primero sueño. Edición de la Universidad de Buenos Aires (Buenos Aires, 1953).

SECONDARY SOURCES

1. Books

ABREU GÓMEZ, ERMILO. *Poesías de Juana Inés de la Cruz,* 2a. ed. (México: Ediciones Botas, 1948). Read the long prologue, an important thesis that has carried much subsequent criticism in its train. The author argues that Sor Juana was Cartesian in her thought and that she did not have a religious vocation: she deceived the State and Church of her time for her own intellectual ends.

ARROYO, ANITA. *Razón y pasión de Sor Juana* (México: Ed. Porrúa y Obregón, 1952). A rationalist interpretation of Sor Juana. The author follows the thesis of Abreu Gómez and sees Sor Juana as a rebellious woman who entered the convent for mundane reasons.

CHÁVEZ, EZEQUIEL. *Ensayo de psicología de Sor Juana Inés de la Cruz* (Barcelona: Editorial Araluce, 1931). Pictures Sor Juana as a disembodied spirit who flies to the Great Beyond. A pantheistic interpretation that modernizes Sor Juana.

FERNANDEZ MACGREGOR, GENARO. *La santificación de Sor Juana Inés de la Cruz* (México: Editorial Cultura, 1932). Applies the pantheism of the East to Sor Juana.

GARCÉS, JESÚS JUAN. *Vida y poesía de Sor Juana Inés de la Cruz* (Madrid: Ediciones Cultura Hispánica, 1953). Applies the impressionism of Azorín to Sor Juana. This book is similar to Azorín's *Al margen de los clásicos.*

JIMÉNEZ RUEDA, JULIO. *Sor Juana Inés de la Cruz en su época* (México: Editorial Porrúa, 1951). A brief biography of Sor Juana.

JUNCO, ALFONSO. *Gente de México* (México: Ediciones Botas, 1937). Contains valuable criticism of other critics of Sor Juana. A historical study of Sor Juana.

MÉNDEZ PLANCARTE, ALFONSO and SALCEDA, ALBERTO G. *Obras completas de Sor Juana Inés de la Cruz* 4 vols. (México: Fondo de Cultura Económica, 1951-1957). Méndez Plancarte is the foremost critic of Sor Juana. His notes are indispensable.

MENÉNDEZ PELAYO, MARCELINO. *Historia de la poesía hispanoamericana,* Vol. I. (Santander: Aldus, S. A. de Artes Gráficas, 1948). 67-76. A good description of Sor Juana's works.

NERVO, AMADO. *Juana de Asbaje: Obras completas de Amado Nervo,* Vol. VIII. (Madrid: Biblioteca Nueva, 1910). Good criticism of Sor Juana's poetry by a famous poet.

PFANDL, LUDWIG. *Sor Juana Inés de la Cruz. La décima musa de México: Su vida, su poesía, su psique* (Mexico: Universidad Nacional Autónoma de México, 1963). A Freudian interpretation of Sor Juana.

WALLACE, ELIZABETH. *Sor Juana Inés de la Cruz, Poetisa de corte y convento* (México: Ediciones Xochitl, 1944). Accepts a great deal of the Abreu Gómez school but does not oppose Sor Juana to the Church so much.

2. Articles

BLANCO AGUINAGA, CARLOS. "Dos sonetos del siglo XVI: Amor-locura en Quevedo y Sor Juana," *Modern Language Notes,* LXXVII, 145-61. Argues that two sonnets of Quevedo and Sor Juana surprise the reader since both authors are carried away by poetical intuitions contrary to those truths on which their entire existence and works are based.

DURAN, MANUEL. "El drama intelectual de Sor Juana y el anti-intelectualismo hispánico," *Cuadernos Americanos,* Año XXII, CXXIX, 238-53. Argues that Sor Juana's spirit was "inclined to a certain relativism." Studies the problem of anti-feminism and concludes that Sor Juana's character, although feminine and emotional, was essentially rationalist.

FLYNN, GERARD. "The Alleged Mysticism of Sor Juana Inés de la Cruz," *Hispanic Review*, XXVIII, 233-44. Argues that Sor Juana is not a mystic.

————. "A Revision of the Philosophy of Sor Juana Inés de la Cruz," *Hispania*, XLIII, 515-20. Argues that Sor Juana's philosophy is Scholastic rather than Cartesian.

————. "The *Primero sueño* of Sor Juana Inés de la Cruz," *Revista Interamericana de Bibliografía*, XV (1965), 355-59. Argues that *The Dream* of Sor Juana is two poems rather than one.

LEAL, LUIS. "El 'Tocotín mestizo' de Sor Juana," *Abside*, XVIII, 51-64. A brief study of the philological value of the *villancicos* of Sor Juana. Discusses the *tocotín*, the song and dance of the Indians, in the St. Peter Nolasco *villancicos* of 1677.

LEONARD, IRVING. "The *encontradas correspondencias* of Sor Juana Inés," *Hispanic Review*, XXIII. Argues that Sor Juana, "an ambivalent personality of feminine emotion and masculine intellectuality," had a profound internal conflict. Hers was a distraught nature and she could not reciprocate the love of the Church for her. Three of her sonnets make use of *encontradas correspondencias*, or triangular antitheses, which reflect her own unhappy state.

PEMAN, JOSÉ MARIA. "Sinceridad y artificio en la poesía de Sor Juana Inés de la Cruz," *Homenaje a Sor Juana . . . de la Real Academia Española* (Madrid: S. Aguirre, impresor, 1952). Introduces the question of Spanish *senequismo* (Seneca-ism) into Sor Juana criticism. Denies that Sor Juana was a mystic.

PUCCINI, DARIO. "Los villancicos de Sor Juana Inés de la Cruz," *Cuadernos Americanos*, Año XXIV (1965), CXLII, 223-52. Studies the structural originality of Sor Juana's *villancicos* and their relation to the other works of Sor Juana. Very well documented.

————. *Sor Juana Inés de la Cruz. Studio d'una personalità del Barocco messicano.* Edizioni dell'Ateneo, Roma 1967. This study throws light on the *Respuesta a Sor Filotea* episode, explains the allegorical elements in Sor Juana's poetry, and examines her *villancicos*.

RIVERS, ELIAS. "El ambiguo *Sueño* de Sor Juana," *Cuadernos hispanoamericanos*, LXIII. 271-82. Argues that the *Sueño* is a poem with philosophical overtones. The example of Phaeton, who went down to glorious defeat, is symbolical of Sor Juana's intellectual career.

SALINAS, PEDRO. "En busca de Juana de Asbaje" in *Memoria del Segundo Congreso Internacional de Catedráticos de Literatura Iberoamericana* (Berkeley, 1941). Argues that Sor Juana's poetry was only an imitation, owing to the spiritual climate of the

Mexican court. Not a born poet, not a born nun, Sor Juana had a tremendous intellectual drive of knowledge for the sake of knowledge.

SCHONS, DOROTHY. "Some Obscure Points in the Life of Sor Juana Inés de la Cruz," *Modern Philology*, November 1926. Argues that there were sinister and fanatical elements in the Church, which persecuted Sor Juana. Opens the way to the criticism of Abreu Gómez.

VOSSLER, KARL. "El Mundo en el Sueño," in *Primero Sueño* Buenos Aires: Edición de la Universidad de Buenos Aires, 1953). Argues that *The Dream* is a masterpiece. Writes a prose transcription of *The Dream*.

————. "La Décima Musa de México," in *Obras escogidas de Sor Juana* (Buenos Aires: Colección Austral, 1946). Argues that Sor Juana's age was a period of decline, a twilight age. It is customary at such a time for brilliant personalities (such as Sor Juana) to emerge. For Sor Juana the Baroque program of "surprise and be surprised" was instinctual. Denies that Sor Juana was a mystic.

Index

Abreu Gómez, Ermilo, 34, 120
Alonso, Dámaso, 111
Aquinas, St. Thomas, 17, 27, 34, 110
Aristotle, 27-28, 34, 96, 110, 113
Augustine, St., 17
auto sacramental, 53, 56, 68, 76, 103, 113-14
Azorín (José Martínez Ruiz), 118

Bacchus, 31
Baroque art, 29, 120
Black inclination of Sor Juana, 18-22
Black legend of Sor Juana, 13, 99

Calderón, Pedro, 11-13, 28-29, 32, 37, 42-43, 45, 51, 68-71, 76-77, 108-09, 111-15
Carmelites, 16
Carta atenagórica (The Letter Worthy of Minerva), 18, 24
Castro Leal, Antonio, 109
Catherine of Egypt, Ste., 23
Celestina, 39
Cervantes, Miguel de, 52, 113
Charles II, 14, 108
Charles V, 14
Chávez, Ezequiel, 34, 99
Christ, 18, 23, 28, 57, 60, 62, 64, 68, 72, 74, 76, 78, 80, 88
Chrysostom, St. John, 17

Cicero, 50, 113
Comedia, 76-77; *comedia de enredo*, 36-38, 41, 46-47, 49, 51-52
Cotarelo y Mori, Emilio, 112
Crisógono, Padre, 100

Descartes, René, 34, 117
Díaz del Castillo, Bernal, 12
discursive reasoning, 28, 33
Divine Narcissus, The (auto sacramental), 12, 35, 56-74, 78, 81, 96, 98, 104, 108
Dream, The, 19, 26-35, 95-96, 98, 108, 119, 120

Epistemology, 26, 34
Etchegoyen, Gaston, 101, 116
Eusebius, 23
Exaltation of nature, 30-31, 33
Exegesis, 23

Fernández de Santa Cruz, Manuel, bishop of Puebla, 18, 24
Filotea, Sor (pseudonym of the bishop of Puebla), 18-20, 24
Freud, Sigmund, 118

Garcilaso de la Vega, el Inca, 12
Gertrude, Ste., 23
Gil Polo, Gaspar, 13
Gilson, Étienne, 110, 116

Góngora, Don Luis de, 11, 30, 33-34, 108, 111
Gracioso, 37-38, 40, 42, 46-47, 52, 109, 112
Gregory the Great, 75
Guevara, Juan de, 45

Hanke, Lewis, 113
Harmony of faith and reason, 24-25, 108, 110
Harvey, William, 34
Hermenegildo, St., 74-78, 104
Hieronymites, 16
Hopkins, Gerard Manley, 115-16

Incident of the letters, 17-25
Indian mutiny, 16, 24
Inquisition, 22
Intellectual, intellectual liberty, 19, 24, 108
Intuition, 26-29, 67

James II, 16
Jerome, St., 18
Jesuits, 13, 17, 24
John of the Cross, St., 62-63, 100-102, 105
Joseph's Scepter, 78-81, 98
Juana Inés de la Cruz, Sor, biography, 11-25
Just war, 74

Kircher, Athanasius, 34

La Boetie, Étienne, 50
Las Casas, Bartolomé de la, 74
Last years, 24
Latin, 15, 20
Letter From Sor Filotea de la Cruz, 18
Letter to the Corinthians, 25
Ley, Charles David, 109, 112
Loa, 53, 56, 69, 72-74, 77, 96-97, 103

Lope de Vega, 51-52, 76-77, 105, 112
Love The Greater Labyrinth, 12, 45-52
Lovejoy, Arthur O., 110, 112
Luis de León, Fray, 39
Lull, Raymond, 101-2
Lyrical poetry, 88-95

Mancera, marquesa de, 15
Mariana, Juan de, 114
Martyr of the Sacrament, The, 74-78, 81
Mary, Virgin, 24, 61, 64, 66, 68, 83, 86, 98
Méndez Plancarte, Alfonso, 11, 33-34, 89, 99-100, 103-5
Menéndez Pelayo, Marcelino, 11, 34, 88, 111, 114, 116
Menéndez Pidal, Ramon, 116
Metaphysics, 18, 28
Mojiganga, 45, 112
Montaigne, Michel de, 50, 113
Monterde, Francisco, 111-13
Moreto, Diego de, 43
Mulieres in ecclesia taceant, 18-19, 23
Mysticism, 99-107, 116, 119

Nature in Sor Juana's poetry, 95-98
Navarro Tomás, Tomás, 111
Negro poetry, 82-88, 114
Nervo, Amado, 99
Núñez, Padre, 24

Ovid, 31-32, 95

Pascal, Blaise, 28-29
Paul, St., 18, 23, 25
Paula, Ste., 23
Pfandl, Ludwig, 11, 34, 109
Pirandello, Luigi, 45
Plato, 34

Primacy of faith, 22, 24-25
Primacy of reason, 25
Pundonor, 38, 41

Quevedo, Francisco de, 118

Religious vocation, 16, 10-21
Reply to Sor Filotea, The, 14-24,
    26, 35, 74, 102-3, 108
Robles, Antonio de, 109
Rojas Zorrilla, Francisco de, 43,
    51, 112
Rudolph, Emperor, 14
Rulfo, Juan, 12

Sainete, 42-44, 45, 54
Salinas, Pedro, 111
Salvation, 21, 24-25
Sarao of the Four Nations, 54
Scholasticism, 28, 33, 40, 88, 95-
    98, 110, 119
Senequismo, 119
Sepúlveda, Juan Ginés de, 74
Sertillanges, R. P., 110
Shaw, George Bernard, 12
Sicroff, Albert A., 115

Silva, 31-32
Song of Songs, 19, 61-62, 101
Suárez, Francisco, 74, 113

Textual control of the imagina-
    tion, 13, 24
Theology, 21, 24, 34
Theresa of Avila, Ste., 23, 100-
    103
Trials of a Noble House, The, 35-
    42, 51-52, 59, 68, 103, 108

Usigli, Rodolfo, 12

Valbuena Prat, Angel, 76-77
Viceroys, 15, 53, 108
Vieyra, Antonio de, 17, 19, 108
Villancicos, 17, 55, 74, 82-88, 103,
    119
Vitoria, Francisco de, 74
Vossler, Karl, 34

Writing at the behest of others,
    19, 26, 55, 74, 89

Yáñez, Agustín, 12